COMEDY
ACTING FOR
THEATRE

COMEDY ACTING FOR THEATRE

The Art and Craft of Performing in Comedies

SIDNEY HOMAN
AND
BRIAN RHINEHART

Bloomsbury Academic
An imprint of Bloomsbury Publishing Plc

B L O O M S B U R Y
LONDON · OXFORD · NEW YORK · NEW DELHI · SYDNEY

Bloomsbury Methuen Drama

An imprint of Bloomsbury Publishing Plc

Imprint previously known as Methuen Drama

50 Bedford Square	1385 Broadway
London	New York
WC1B 3DP	NY 10018
UK	USA

www.bloomsbury.com

BLOOMSBURY, METHUEN DRAMA and the Diana logo are trademarks of Bloomsbury Publishing Plc

First published 2018

British Library Cataloguing-in-Publication Data
A catalogue record for this book is available from the British Library.

ISBN: HB: 978-1-3500-1276-9
PB: 978-1-3500-1277-6
ePDF: 978-1-3500-1275-2
eBook: 978-1-3500-1278-3

Library of Congress Cataloging-in-Publication Data
A catalog record for this book is available from the Library of Congress.

Series: Performance Books

Cover design: Holly Bell

Typeset by Newgen KnowledgeWorks Pvt. Ltd., Chennai, India
Printed and bound in India

To find out more about our authors and books visit www.bloomsbury.com. Here you will find extracts, author interviews, details of forthcoming events, and the option to sign up for our newsletters.

To Norma and Alev

CONTENTS

PERMISSION ACKNOWLEDGMENTS

Chapter 1

Extracts from Yasmina Reza, *"Art"* © Yasmina Reza (author) and Christopher Hampton (translator), 1996, used with permission of Faber and Faber Ltd.

Excerpts from *"Art"* by Yasmina Reza, translated by Christopher Hampton. Copyright © 1994 by Yasmina Reza. Translation © 1996 by Yasmina Reza and Christopher Hampton. Reprinted with permission of Farrar, Straus and Giroux.

Chapter 2

Extract from Molière, *Tartuffe*, © Dover Publications, Inc., 2000, used with permission.

Chapter 3

Dinner by Moira Buffini (© Moira Buffini, 2002) is printed with permission of United Agents (www.unitedagents.co.uk) on behalf of Moira Buffini.

Chapter 4

Extracts from *Beyond Therapy* reprinted with permission of Helen Merrill LLC. Copyright © 1981 by Christopher Durang.

Chapter 5

Chapter 6

Chapter 7

Chapter 8

INTRODUCTION

Stage comedy is not just telling jokes. It's about creating characters that audiences perceive as funny, characters who may be totally unaware of their absurdity or only dimly so. They may even consider themselves funny in ways that have nothing to do with the reaction from the audience. One thing is certain—the truly comic character is never ever just trying to get a laugh. Warren Beatty has said that one of his most demanding roles was as the washed-up comedian in Arthur Penn's 1965 film *Mickey One*. Beatty's character thinks he is still funny onstage, sees himself as an engaging performer but, from the audience's perspective, both in the film itself and in the movie theatre, he is funny only because he is so bad—an unconscious parody of all comedians desperate to get a laugh and yet not realizing how awful they really are.[1]

Comedy differs from tragedy in its view of humanity, in the way it is structured, in the range of its dialogue, and in the various styles of acting it requires, not to mention the subject matter. But it still is *about* something, its characters not unlike those on the darker side of the stage. It is notable that Samuel Beckett, the benchmark playwright of our modern theatre, subtitled his most famous play, *Waiting for Godot*, a "tragicomedy." And that, toward the culmination of his career, Shakespeare himself turned to the tragicomedy genre with his latter plays—*Pericles*, *Cymbeline*, *The Winter's Tale*, and, most magnificently, *The Tempest*.

Comedies end happily, tragedies unhappily—or so the earnest high-school English teacher would have us believe. This simple contrast, however, leaves out a lot. By taking action that he knows will possibly result in death, doesn't our tragic hero gain stature, see himself in a broader perspective and, in doing so, discover a measure of joy?

Similarly, characters in comedy may be lovable or less than lovable, clumsy in society, and ignorant to the degree that we want to strangle them, and yet they are also capable of change, of vision, however limited. Thus, comedy's so-called happy endings often come at a price: compromises sometimes must be made, the ideal is reduced to the real, characters are forced to face the fact that they are not who they thought they were—are perhaps not as noble, as bright, or even as attractive.

What happens when we see humans as something less than Hamlets or Macbeths, as sometimes pathetic, foolish, or frustratingly unaware of themselves or their world? We see they are worthy of our attention, not just our laughter; perhaps, in them we see something of ourselves. In this book, we examine what it takes to be a good comic actor, to do justice to a genre that embraces humor, satire, parody, or farce, from one-liners to a more sustained view of the human condition. We explore the best principles and "rules" for the comedic actor, and examine how acting exercises or improv techniques can help too. Comedy is viewed in terms of the stage, as something transpiring between actor and audience, rather than simply as a piece of literature.

The book's subtitle, *The Art and Craft of Performing in Comedies*, sets the boundaries for our inquiry. On the one hand, we treat comedy as an "art," an aesthetic form that, to a *degree*, can be subjected to a literary-like analysis: its plot, structure, characterization, language—its meaning. Therein, the play, to a *degree*, exists before the playwright takes it to the company, before it undergoes enactment by actors and the director. And a good playwright will surely have this destination in mind, this movement from the study to the stage, and accordingly will put in stage directions, character notes, perhaps even suggestions to the lighting and design staff—and, if the playwright is Harold Pinter, lots of pauses; if it is Samuel Beckett, lots of silence. However, it's the other word in the subtitle that gets our main focus: "craft," a skill that can be taught, mastered, and enhanced, as well as all the elements that go into a performance—delivery, pacing, comic timing, dialogue, movement on stage, adding subtext to a character, gestures, the ways the actor controls his face and voice, and the way his body shows his attitude toward the audience, knowing that they are the ultimate recipients of his craft.[2]

Audiences and general readers alike will find this inquiry both revealing and fun. We have undertaken the improv exercises featured in the book with a variety of groups, from executives to prisoners, from students in China to university faculty—and we suggest you try them too. We look at scenes from a wide variety of plays as if we were a director or fellow actor sitting down with the reader, going over the scenes he is about to play—or might like to play. How does the comedy work? How might the actor shape the comic character? What should he consider in terms of delivery, timing, gesture, movement, or subtext (what the character is thinking to himself just below the dialogue, the inner voice that shapes what he says on stage)? As the actor takes to the stage, where is the character "coming from," both literally and psychologically? What is his history? How does the actor work onstage with other members of the cast? Throughout *Comedy Acting for Theatre*, we refer mostly to plays we've done, as actors or directors, as well as citing various comedians, actors, and directors, along with critics and commentators past and present.

We start where comedy itself starts—and ends, for that matter. With Chapter 1, we turn first to the physiognomy of laughing. Which parts of the brain are involved in the loop from processing the material (the joke, the situation, the character) that makes us laugh and then triggering the response itself? Which parts of the body are involved in that response? We also explore the case for laughter as a homeostasis activity, one that helps preserve our physical and mental well-being.

Then we turn to "why," using observations and theories from social scientists, sociologists, psychologists, psychiatrists, and most certainly philosophers—Hobbes, Kant, Kierkegaard, Schopenhauer, Spencer, Bergson—as well as contemporary theorists, including other authors of books for the comic actor. By way of illustration, we look at Christopher Hampton's translation of Yasmina Reza's *"Art,"* a play in which a friend's laughter at a painting ignites a series of events.

Chapters 2–6 are something of an actor's manual—how to do it. In Chapter 2, our focus is on improvisation (improv) as a way of enhancing an actor's feel for, or his ability to do, comedy improv both as a rehearsal device and as a supplement to the script during the run of the play. How can the director use improv to explore the skills and the personalities of his actors and find ways to sharpen the comedy itself? These improvs and games offer both a way of exploring why we laugh and an overture to the book's subsequent chapters.

Chapter 3 discusses the basic principles or "rules" of comedy, with inserts for improv activities to make the advice more immediate. The rules encompass character analysis/history (in conjunction with which, for example, we offer an improv called "character interview"), playing obstacles, clarity of expression, body awareness, joke structure and comic timing, natural versus stylized acting, and the relationship between one's self and one's comic character. We supplement the general discussion with commentators, both ancient and modern. Then we apply these seven rules to the seven characters in Moira Buffini's black comedy, *Dinner*.

In Chapter 4, these rules for the comic actor are coupled with elements of the comic character. Here, we look at over- and underreacting, playing incongruity and opposites (in the character), applied childishness, rapidly changing emotions, hypervulnerability, status shifts, collapses of dignity, and self-ignorance. To make the elements specific, we look at them in relation to Christopher Durang's *Beyond Therapy* and John Pielmeier's short plays *Cheek to Cheek* and *Goober's Descent*.

In Chapter 5, the discussion expands to what we consider to be the larger "psychological and performance issues in playing comedy." How does the comic actor keep up his commitment night after night? How can he infuse even more depth to his character, especially if he senses his character is getting dull or, worse yet, shallow? Our topics here incorporate energy and intensity, self-confidence/relaxation, and a spirit of play. What have recent actors, directors, critics said about these topics? And how might the comic actor apply them to his character? We first deliberate these questions as they pertain to one of the best examples of a comedy demanding energy and intensity — David Lindsay-Abaire's *Wonder of the World*. Then, we pursue the four topics through a very different play, Harold Pinter's "review sketch," *Last to Go*.

Next, building on the issues explored in Chapters 2–5, we examine a whole play scene by scene, as good comic actors fashion their role on a character's progress through the play, seeing growth in terms of a through-line or "arc." Moreover, in Chapter 6, we look at Michael Frayn's *Noises Off*, probably one of the most popular physical comedies, and one very much about the theatre.

In Chapter 7, we turn to the master playwright and show what variations comedy can take in five of his plays, as well as the options afforded for playing the comic characters. When an actor does a Shakespearean comedy, he experiences both the similarities and the differences between classic and modern comedies. In this chapter, we look at *The Comedy of Errors*; of course, the Kate–Petruchio duel from *The Taming of the Shrew*; that comic trio of Maria, Sir Toby, and Sir Andrew in *Twelfth Night*; the "kill Claudio" scene from *Much Ado about Nothing*; and perhaps the Shakespearean comedy to end all comedies, the wretchedly funny production of *Pyramus and Thisbe* from *A Midsummer Night's Dream*.

Finally, in Chapter 8, we work with four recent plays: Richard Bean's farce *One Man, Two Guvnors*, the playwright's reworking of the Carlo Goldoni classic *The Servant of Two Masters*; the physical comedy *The Play That Goes Wrong* by Henry Lewis, Jonathan Sayer, and Henry Shields; a prototype of what might be called sentimental or romantic comedy, Tim Firth's *Calendar Girls*; and Nick Payne's social, political comedy *The Same Deep Water as Me*. Correspondingly, we present four different approaches for the actor to consider, covering getting into the world of farce, doing physical comedy, establishing a basis for a character in the opening scene, and evaluating objectives and subtext for the comic actor.

Our approach to acting comedy, ranging from the academic and theoretical to the practical, reflects our parallel but somewhat divergent careers. One of your authors, Brian Rhinehart, works in New York's professional theatres as an actor and director, and then brings his experience to students in the Actors Studio Drama School at Pace University. The other, Sidney Homan, professor of English at the University of Florida, is the author of numerous books on Shakespeare and the modern playwrights that grow out of his own work on commercial and university stages. We have acted in each other's productions in formal theatres as well as venues ranging from prisons to bars, and have worked together as writers and actors in the improv and sketch-comedy group, Theatre Strike Force. To simplify presentation, throughout this book, we use the plural "we" when citing works we have done individually, whether as actors or directors, for, while not of one mind in all things, we find that in most aspects of the theatre we are in agreement.

Notes

1. See Bosley Crowther, review of *Mickey One*, *New York Times*, September 9, 1965, http://movies.nytimes.com/movie/review?res=9F01E 5D91130E23ABC4153DFBF66838E679EDEhttp://movies.nytimes.com/ movie/review?res=9F01E5D91130E23ABC4153DFBF66838E679EDE (accessed July 5, 2011).
2. With a few exceptions, the generic masculine pronoun "he" and its derived forms are used in the text to stand for either sex.

1
WHY WE LAUGH

With laughter, we challenge reason through our imagination, as we collaborate with the joke-teller in the illusory, transitory world created by the playwright, director, and actors. For Paul Grice, we laugh at "fantasies as if they were reasonable hypotheses."[1] With laughter, we experience what has been termed a "cognitive shift,"[2] moving from what comedians call "the set-up" toward a new situation, be it a punch line or comic resolution. For this reason, humor is said to be "aesthetic ... to the extent that the cognitive shift is enjoyed for its own sake, playfully, and not for any boon that it signals."[3] Comedy has something in common with the laughing Buddha: the idea of non-attachment, freedom from rigid principles, from systems. Like the Buddha, we laugh at the world as a way of maintaining our own integrity, of avoiding the inevitability of tragedy.

Laughter is both the tool of the comedic actor and the goal of the comedy itself. Whether a guffaw at a joke or a reflective chuckle greeting a sarcastic remark, laughter is the audience's means of ratifying the performance and collaborating in its meaning. So, let's start at the beginning, exploring this mutuality. Back to basics, then: What happens when we laugh and why do we laugh?

Laughter is something real, not theoretical—it's there, witnessed by both the comedic actor and the audience, even on an MRI of the brain. Betty Vine, in her article "The Neuroscience of Comedy,"[4] cited a study in which participants viewed episodes of *Seinfeld* and *The Simpsons* and neuroscientists "detected a two-part detection and appreciation process" when audience members laughed:

Joke detection occurred in the left inferior frontal and posterior temporal cortices on the left side of the brain. After our brains perceive the joke, our amygdales release a spate of dopamine, and, in turn, neurons called spindle cells further assist in the funny-making monkey business by transmitting the delighted emotion across the brain.

It's the brain's frontal lobes that allow us to grasp (and laugh at) the "discrepancy between the script and the situation described by the joke."[5] As Caitlin Kirkwood described on her blog *The Synaptic Scoop*, the brain, so alerted, then sends a message to the facial muscles, "pulling the corners of your lips upward and backward, and narrowing your eyes."[6] With the muscles in the respiratory system and the voice box now activated, the product is laughter—also known as "an involuntary, rhythmic vocalization."[7]

We enter the theatre with our brain full of assumed scenarios about the world, the memories with which we make assumptions or take action when confronted with similar situations. If a comic situation or performance (even a single joke delivered by a stand-up comedian) surprises us, as long as it makes sense on its own terms—however unnatural or bizarre the situation—we accept it and enjoy the humor without worrying about how improbable it might be.

Christopher Hampton's translation of Yasmina Reza's *"Art"* is a fitting illustration because it is a comedy about laughing.[8] The title itself signals a double function of comedy. On the one hand, its "art" lies in the commitment of the comic actor to a character obsessed with a false interpretation of both art and friendship that, in time, will be wonderfully and joyfully dispelled—after all, this is what comedy does. But, until its resolution, the three characters in *"Art"* take laughing seriously. Calling his purchase absurd and downright elitist, Marc laughs at Serge's paying an exorbitant price for a painting by the artist Antrios: "You paid two hundred thousand francs for this shit?"[9] Their mutual friend Yvan tries to play the peacemaker. Marc's laughter, taken in dead seriousness by the two combatants, is the lynchpin for the audience's response to the comedy. Once the three friends can laugh along with us, can in a sense bond with the audience, the conflict can be resolved.

A neurologist, Richard Restak, has posited that this resolution depends on "the deep relationship that exits in the human brain between the laughable and the illogical."[10] If the comedy is well-made and well-staged, the brain filters out irrelevant material so that we relish the situation, the joke. However, people with injuries to the frontal lobe cannot "shift back and forth between an initial assumption ... and the alternative explanation suggested by a joke."[11] Laughter is a healthy, restorative response, defined as a "homeostatic mechanism by which psychological tension is reduced," allowing "biological systems to maintain relatively constant conditions in the internal environment."[12]

Look at the following scene in *"Art"* where Yvan tells Marc of his meeting with Serge. It is a challenge to the two actors playing characters because they are operating by what Immanuel Kant called two different, competing scripts,[13] or what Victor Raskin saw as the process of substituting one semantic "script" for another[14]—here, two very different interpretations of the same meeting, albeit one firsthand and the other only reported.

Yvan We laughed.

Marc You laughed?

Yvan We laughed. Both of us. We laughed. I promise you on Catherine's life, we had a good laugh, both of us, together.

Marc You told him it was shit and you had a good laugh.

Yvan No, I didn't tell him it was shit, we laughed spontaneously.

Marc You arrived, you looked at the painting and you laughed. And then he laughed.

Yvan Yes. Something like that. We talked a little and then it was pretty much the way you described it.

Marc And it was a genuine laugh.

Yvan Perfectly genuine.

Marc Well, then, I've made a mistake. Good. I'm really pleased to hear it.

Yvan It was even better than you think. It was Serge who laughed first.

Marc It was Serge who laughed first . . .

Yvan Yes.

Marc He laughed first and you joined in.

Yvan Yes.

Marc But what made him laugh?

Yvan He laughed because he sensed I was about to laugh. I guess he laughed to put me at my ease.

Marc It doesn't count if he laughed fist. If he laughed first it was to defuse your laughter. I mean it wasn't a genuine laugh.

Yvan It was a genuine laugh.

> **Marc**   It might have been a genuine laugh, but it wasn't for the right reason.
>
> **Yvan**   What is the right reason? I'm confused.
>
> **Marc**   He wasn't laughing because his painting is ridiculous, you and he weren't laughing for the same reason, you were laughing at the painting and he was laughing to ingratiate himself, to put himself on your wavelength, to show that on top of being an aesthete who can spend more on a painting than you earn in a year, he's still the same old rebellious pal you used to kid around with.[15]

For Yvan, laughter is innocent, possibly restorative, a way to change how Marc thinks of Serge. Marc, in contrast, sees language—in particular, the word "laughter"—as at best a tool, at worst a weapon—a means of concealing one's true objective (if Serge's was a "genuine laugh," it wasn't for "the right reason"). In his discourse on *Human Nature*, Thomas Hobbes argues that laughter expresses our need in a competitive society to feel superior: "The passion of laughter is nothing else but sudden glory arising from some sudden conception of some eminency in ourselves."[16] Marc sees Serge as "an aesthete who can spend more on a painting than [Ivan earns] in a year," someone projecting a false image to hide the "old rebellious pal [Ivan] used to kid around with."

With "laughed" and "laughing" so pervasive—the words occur twenty-four times!—the two actors might want to make its every occurrence uniquely their own, both in delivery and the subtext. After a few rehearsals, it might be productive to have the actors switch parts, thereby underscoring the other's choices so they can get into the heads of the opposite character whose script is chained to the meaning of laughter. The actor must be cognizant that the source of this quarrel about the price we put on art, especially modernist art, is inseparable from the fear that Serge values the painting more than their fifteen-year friendship.

Laughter is a behavior rooted in our daily conversations, our interactions with one another, whether pleasant or unpleasant, a "function," as Norman Holland established in his book on laughing, "of [our individual] identity."[17] For Anthony Ludovici, laughter comes when "we feel that our adaption to life is superior."[18] As we will maintain throughout this book, the comic character doesn't see himself as comic; he holds his view of the world, however absurd, with absolute seriousness and sincerity. The irony in *"Art"* is that, until its resolution, the three characters in the play take laughing seriously—too seriously.

Serge brands Marc's response "a real know it all laugh."[19] Later, he describes Marc's "sardonic laugh" as having "not a trace of charm"[20] when he dismisses the painting as a "grotesque joke."[21] Branding Serge an "aesthete"[22] who celebrates "deconstruction," Marc is even disturbed by his pronouncing that word "humorously, unapologetically, without a trace of irony."[23] And he tells Yvan that, while Serge used to be "a freak with a sense of humor," now what really upsets him is that "you can't laugh with him anymore"; Yvan, though, declares that he will "make him laugh."[24] At Yvan's intervention, when Serge asks him if the purchase is "crazy or what," Yvan replies "crazy," and the stage direction calls for *"Hearty laughter. They stop. They look at each other. They start again."*[25]

The French philosopher Henri Bergson set forth several conditions for laughter, all based on the principle of incongruity: the inability of the source of the laughter to conform to society's expectations; the absence of emotion, which Bergson found incompatible with the role of the laugher; and the laugher's ability to reduce the person laughed at to a "thing." He added, "What is essentially laughable is what is done automatically."[26] For the nineteenth-century German philosopher Arthur Schopenhauer, two extremes produce this humorous incongruity: the mismatch between abstract categories and particular instances of those categories.[27] In his analysis of humor and laughter, linguist Wallace Chafe offered an example from Schopenhauer of an actor in Berlin who was forbidden to improvise by his director. On one occasion, when he appeared onstage riding a horse, the animal defecated, to which the actor wittily rejoined: "Don't you know we're forbidden to improvise?"[28]

This incongruity, a source of tension, led the English philosopher Herbert Spencer, and others, to see laughter as a "discharge of tension."[29] Our laughter as an audience is possible because we are isolated from real harm; the stage comedy, no matter how much based on real life, is just an illusion. For Yvan, laughter is innocent, possibly restorative; a way to change how Marc thinks of Serge. For him, laughter can lead to that dissolution of tension.

But until this happens, Yvan's problems with wedding invitations (he delivers a two-page monologue on the controversy with his relatives), Serge's ex-wife, and his hatred of Marc's wife Paula for the way she smokes cigarettes, the business of art, and the clash between classical and modernist aesthetics all swirl around the little world, the "conditions of conflict"[30] resulting from Marc's "vile pretentious laugh"[31] at an all-white painting. And it is indeed a little world—stage directions call for "*A single set. As stripped down and neutral as possible.*"[32]

When Marc first hears that the laughter was "genuine," he is relieved by Yvan's reply that it was indeed "perfectly genuine" and then confesses to making a "mistake." But, a beat later, he negates himself when he learns that it was Serge who laughed first. What a sudden change in mood—for the character and the actor. For the audience, Marc's interpretation of the meeting at Serge's tells us more about him than anything else. We experience what Robert Latta has called, in his book *The Basic Humor Process*, "relaxation";[33] our laughter is pure, disinterested. If the actor playing Yvan adds a subtext of his frustration at Marc for misinterpreting him—indeed, for denying what he knows to be the truth of that conversation with Serge—we can laugh at this self-tortured soul who thinks he understands what went on better than the actual participants. The more skilled the actors are in taking seriously this inane and ultimately irrelevant exchange on a single word, the more they will let us "feel their pain." The actors can involve us, even as we in the house are removed from their anxiety, as each frantically pursues his objective: Yvan, to reassure Marc that the quarrel will evaporate; Marc, to confirm his own negative judgment of both the painting and his friend.

There is a serious, understandable human concern behind this argument over the nature of the laughter. Serge, however disingenuously, is trying to restore his reputation as the "old rebellious pal" he used to be. Marc only exposes, even if unconsciously, the real reason he laughed at the Antrios: he fears Serge values the painting more than their friendship, that he's been "betrayed" and "abandoned" for a piece of surreal art.[34] Serge himself puts the question to Marc: "Are you saying, I replaced you with Antrios?" To this, Marc first replies with a single "Yes" and then elaborates, "Yes. With the Antrios … and everything it implies."[35] Again, as Latta suggested, at moments like this, the actor, in giving a convincing illusion that Marc is sincere and committed in his answer, paradoxically allows the audience to relax: it is absurd that a painting could take the place of a friend, especially a painting, there on the set, that is surely a parody of the excesses of modernism. In comedy, we anticipate a resolution, a step beyond absurdity—or, as John Morreall, founder of the International Society for Humor Studies, would have it, we move individually and collectively from a bad situation, however unwarranted, to a better one.[36] Marc's "old rebellious pal," born of his conviction that Serge is trying to steal Yvan, will return at the end of the play.

Serge lets Marc deface the painting with a blue felt-tip marker. And, after the friends have cleaned up and restored the painting "with the aid of Swiss soap plus added ox gall, recommended by Paula,"[37] Marc, whose laugher initiated the conflict, breaks into poetry: he now sees in the painting "a canvas about five feet four ... a man who moves across a space / then disappears."[38]

According to Sigmund Freud, in *Jokes and Their Relation to the Unconscious*, humor displaces the energy we would normally expend on suppressing sexual or aggressive thoughts and feelings; the laugh transfers that energy to a situation that is ultimately found "unnecessary," nonthreatening, fictive.[39] Norman Holland called laughter, as defined by Freud, the "pleasure" we receive "by an economy of psychic expenditure in inhibition."[40]

There may be a curious parallel between our immunity through laughter from the inevitable or tragic and the "V effect" advocated by Brecht, where we, whether actor or audience, are at some psychological distance from the events enacted onstage, and thus in a position to reflect on them and put them in a larger sociological or historical context.[41] However, this V effect, when applied to a joke and manifested in the laugh, is more confined to the audience's immediate experience, even though the events depicted onstage may have parallels and thus relevance to what transpires outside the theatre.

This release of tension, at one with our release of energies otherwise expended in psychic repression, has been linked to the concept of "vitalism," to what is natural, romantic, uninhibited, and free—a force that humorist Sir Jonathan Miller contrasted with "mechanical life."[42] Laughter is the product of our successful struggle against social restrictions. Baldly, it represents a victory of life over death, a force at one with the energies that revive society. The Canadian literary critic and theorist Northrop Frye contended that

The ritualistic pattern behind the catharsis of comedy is the resur-
rection that follows the death ... [and thus] the resolution of New
Comedy is one in which the struggle and rebirth of a divine hero has
shrunk into a marriage, the freeing of a slave, and the triumph of a
young man over an old one.[43]

Laughter thereby signals the resurgence of what is natural and deeply
embedded in the culture over whatever is artificial or suppressive.

With laughter, we move, individually or collectively, from one
situation—threatening, impossible, annoying—to another and better
one, whether the latter serves as a parody of the original situation, a
release from tension, or the assertion of what we know is right or think
is better for us. Morreall cites the television comedian Steve Allen for
whom "tragedy plus time equal comedy."[44]

We know from the start that the situation is not real—it is ripe for
exploitation, a set-up awaiting the punch line. We are sure that, however
much the situation, joke, or comic character may reflect real-life prototypes
or possibilities, they are ultimately about nothing and are only a means to
an end circumscribed and endorsed by our laughter. The comedy may
also have a larger meaning, making a serious comment on life outside
the theatre, but it is external to what is presently onstage before us. The
immediacy of the situation onstage allows our laughter to be pure; the
purpose of what we witness is not to instruct but to evoke laughter.

This is why the comic actor needs to signal to the audience that what
he is doing or saying is not serious. The court jester sends this play
signal by his very costume, before he utters a single word. The comic
actor elicits laughter from what his character takes as dead serious, as
real, but what we know is absurd and an illusion. Our laughter grows
out of the actor's over- or underreacting to what the character thinks is
fact. The comic character pursues what the eighteenth-century novelist
Lawrence Sterne would call a "hobbyhorse"—an agenda, a philosophy,
a conviction, a desire that the character embraces so fervently, so
passionately, that he establishes, unwittingly, a disconnect with the
audience.

Morreall posited that laughter differs from other emotions that are a
"direct adaptation to dangers and opportunities"; it "does not involve
the cognitive and practical engagement of beliefs, desires, and adaptive
actions."[45] Echoing him, Chafe spoke of "non-seriousness," a state

wherein we cannot take a stage comedy as threatening, let alone real.[46] As we encounter a situation that appears to be sad, potentially tragic, humorless, or irremediable, we may suspend our disbelief, taking the first stage of a comic situation as offering a character or event that parallels our own real-life experiences, that elicits in us emotions other than the nonserious. The set up, this is to say, pulls us in and engages us, even as we know it is only the first stage, that the ultimate goal of the joke or stage comedy is either laughter, a resolution of the dilemma, or a way out of the blind alley we first encountered. Then, as we move to the second stage, as that second incompatible script dispels or reverses the first, we experience a state of "appraisal."[47] Our initial emotional response, any identification with the character or situation, is checked or cancelled, for we now realize the situation is ludicrous, nonserious. We can laugh with impunity and pleasure. Laughter thereby fails to motivate specific actions, for, the more amused we are, the less capable we are of any action at all. "When afraid or angry, we are ready to run or attack—we've engaged. When we are amused, we may fall down and wet our pants—we're disengaged."[48]

In *"Art,"* the real issue is not how we value a painting, but how we value each other. The comedy is ultimately not about art but about society. That priority is signaled when Serge lets his friend Marc deface the panting, after which the two restore it. In the play's final moments, Marc, in seeing something of value in the Antrios, finds the larger value in friendship, expressing this restorative change of perception in the play's most insistent example of poetry:

> A solitary man glides downhill on his skis.
> The snow is falling.
> It falls until the man disappears back into the landscape.
> My friend Serge, who's one of my oldest friends,
> has bought a painting.
> It's a canvas about five feet by four.
> It represents a man who moves across a space
> then disappears.[49]

The comedy, onstage and off, moves toward what Frye has called our struggle against social restrictions, a freedom from conflict, and a triumph.[50] Or, as one of our theatre majors once said, "I'll take life over art anytime."

* * *

In this chapter, we have discussed both the physiognomy and the philosophy of laughter, a complex and wonderfully human response to a joke, a situation, or a character that involves both the body and the brain. It is a reaction that has many uses, values, and functions in our daily lives, allowing us to cope with misfortune; gain a perspective on what might otherwise be confusing, random, or inexplicable; come to terms with ourselves; ameliorate a bad situation; mock and perhaps even change someone who is out of sync; defend ourselves against a host of petty or darker irritants; and even convert tragedy, or at least absurdity that threatens chaos, into comedy. The list is practically inexhaustible, and this is why we used as a touchstone Christopher Hampton's translation of Yasmina Reza's play *"Art."* Here, laughter is at once the source of a quarrel, a false mirror by which two former friends see each other, and, ultimately, the source of the restoration of their friendship. It is thus a comedy about laughter as both a weapon and medicine.

Knowing what laughter is, where it comes from, what it can do, why we laugh—these are important considerations but, of course, not the whole story. In the next chapter, we turn our attention from the theoretical and philosophical principles, as well as our reflections on laughter as a theme for the playwright, to observable, tangible techniques for producing laughter onstage. The following unscripted performance and acting exercises can be used by actors to prepare for their roles, complement and enhance rehearsals, and even, in the midst of a run, relearn or rekindle the techniques that will help them to be funny before an audience, and, in doing so, collaborate with the playwright and director in the staging of a comedy.

Notes

1 H. Paul Grice, "Logic and Conversation," in *Syntax and Semantics*, vol. 3, *Speech Acts*, ed. Peter Cole and Jerry L. Morgan (New York: Academic Press, 1975), 58.
2 John Morreall, *Comic Relief: A Comprehensive Philosophy of Humor* (Malden, MA: Wiley-Blackwell, 2009), 50.
3 Ibid., 72.

4 Betty Vine, "The Neuroscience of Comedy," *BrainWorld*, March 26, 2015, http://brainworldmagazine.com/neuroscience-of-comedy/#sthash. a7cN3Nkw.dpuf (accessed May 8, 2016).

5 Richard Restak, "Laughter and the Brain," *American Scholar* (Summer 2013), https://theamericanscholar.org/laughter-and-the-brain/#.VytSXT-y6Hs (accessed May 9, 2016).

6 Caitlin Kirkwood, "No Laughing (Gray) Matter: Laughter, the Brain, and Evolution," *The Synaptic Scoop* (blog), June 28, 2014, http://www.synapticscoop.com/?p=582 (accessed May 8, 2016).

7 Ibid.

8 Yasmina Reza, *"Art,"* trans. Christopher Hampton (New York: Dramatists Play Service, 1996).

9 Ibid., 6.

10 Restak, "Laughter and the Brain."

11 Ibid.

12 *The Free Medical Dictionary*, s.v. "homeostasis," http://medical-dictionary. thefreedictionary.com/homeostasis (accessed May 9, 2016).

13 Immanuel Kant, *Critique of Judgment*, in *The Philosophy of Laughter and Humor*, ed. John Morreall (Albany: State University of New York Press, 1987), 47; see also Morreall, *Comic Relief*, 10–11.

14 Victor Raskin, *Semantic Mechanisms of Humor* (Dordrecht: Reidel, 1984), 107–14.

15 Reza, *"Art,"* 15–16.

16 Thomas Hobbes, in *The English Works of Thomas Hobbes of Malmesbury*, vol. 4, *Tripos in Three Discourses: Human Nature, or the Fundamental Elements of Policy Being a Discovery of the Faculties, Acts and Passions of the Soul of a Man*, ed. Sir William Molesworth (Aalen: Scientia, 1962 [1840]), 45–7, cited in Wallace L. Chafe, *The Importance of Not Being Earnest: The Feeling behind Laughter and Humor* (Philadelphia: John Benjamins Publishing, 2007), 141.

17 Norman Norwood Holland, *Laughing: A Psychology of Humor* (Ithaca: Cornell University Press, 1982), 170.

18 Anthony M. Ludovici, *The Secret of Laughter* (New York: Viking Press, 1933), 62; see also Chafe, *The Importance of Not Being Earnest*, 143–4.

19 Reza, *"Art,"* 7.

20 Ibid., 14.

21 Ibid., 35.

22 Ibid., 16.

23 Ibid., 23.

24 Ibid., 11.

25 Ibid., 13.

26 Henri Bergson, *Laughter: An Essay on the Meaning of the Comic*, trans. Cloudesley Brereton and Fred Rothwell (New York: Macmillan, 1911), 139, 146.

27   Arthur Schopenhauer, *The World as Will and Representation*, 2 vols.,
        trans. E. F. J. Payne (Indian Hills, CO: Falcon's Wing Press, 1958), 91–2;
        see also Chafe, *The Importance of Not Being Earnest*, 145–6.

28   Chafe, *The Importance of Not Being Earnest*, 146.

29   Holland, *Laughing*, 49.

30   Reza, *"Art,"* 43.

31   Ibid., 7.

32   Ibid., 4.

33   Robert L. Latta, *The Basic Humor Process: A Cognitive-Shift Theory and
        the Case against Incongruity* (Berlin: Mouton de Gruyter, 1999), 44.

34   Reza, *"Art,"* 40.

35   Ibid.

36   See Morreall, *Comic Relief*, 53.

37   Reza, *"Art,"* 47.

38   Ibid., 48.

39   Chafe, *The Importance of Not Being Earnest*, 70.

40   Holland, *Laughing*, 49.

41   For Brecht's V effect, see W. A. J. Steer, "Brecht's Epic Theatre: Theory
        and Practice," *The Modern Language Review* 63, no. 3 (1968): 637;
        Walter H. Sokel, "Brecht's Concept of Character," *Comparative Drama*
        5, no. 3 (1971): 177–92; Werner Hecht, "The Development of Brecht's
        Theory of Epic Theatre: 1918–1933," *The Tulane Drama Review* 6, no. 1
        (1961): 94–6.

42   Jonathan Miller, "Jokes and Joking," in *Laughing Matters: A Serious Look
        at Humour*, ed. John R. Durant and Jonathan Miller (Harlow: Longman
        Scientific & Technical, 1988), cited in Susan Purdie, *Comedy: The Mastery
        of Discourse* (Toronto: University of Toronto Press, 1993), 152.

43   Northrop Frye, "The Argument of Comedy," in *Comedy: Developments
        in Criticism*, ed. David J. Palmer (London: Macmillan, 1984), 78–9, cited
        in Purdie, *Comedy*, 153. For more on the catharsis of comedy, see
        Aristotle, *Poetics*, in *Criticism: The Major Texts*, ed. Walter Jackson Bate
        (New York: Harcourt Brace & World, 1952); *Tractatus Coislinianus*, trans.
        Lane Cooper, in *Dramatic Theory and Criticism: Greeks to Grotowski*, ed.
        Bernard F. Dukore (New York: Holt, Rinehart and Winston, 1974).

44   Morreall, *Comic Relief*, 53.

45   Ibid., 23.

46   Chafe, *The Importance of Not Being Earnest*, 61–71.

47   Joseph E. LeDoux, *The Emotional Brain: The Mysterious Underpinnings of
        Emotional Life* (New York: Simon & Schuster, 1996), 48–53.

48   Morreall, *Comic Relief*, 31.

49   Reza, *"Art,"* 47–8.

50   Frye, "The Argument of Comedy," cited in Purdie, *Comedy*, 153.

2
IMPROV AND COMEDY

Improv training can be incredibly valuable for the would-be comedy actor. We focus on short-form improvisations (games and exercises) in this chapter, but much can also be learned from long-form exercises such as those in which the actors take the time to create a narrative that is often complex and extensive—but we'll get to that later.

Improv doesn't necessarily help the actor with script analysis, or with producing emotion on the spot, but it does help in recognizing and playing the "given circumstances" of a scene, and with determining the "actions" of a character. It is little wonder that most comedy actors in films and on television have had improv backgrounds: Tina Fey, Amy Poehler, Dan Aykroyd, Chris Farley, Andy Dick, John Belushi, Bill Murray, Phil Hartman, John Candy, Chevy Chase . . . just to name a few.

If you'll allow a broader definition of improv—some might call it loose or even too loose—then, even in a production where improv is not formally used as an exercise complementing the rehearsal or inspired by the script, it can be argued that improv occurs all the time. For example, when an actor devises a subtext for a character, those inner thoughts that are the basis for the line assigned by the playwright—is this not improv in a way?

Improv is outside the script, a way of providing a context for the character, an exercise to loosen up the actor, to prepare him for the demands of the play "proper," whether it be feeling comfortable before the audience or learning how to think on his feet, or enhancing the sense of fun and pleasure that mark a good performance. Improv assists him as he prepares for his role in a comedy, from the moment the actor is assigned his part and begins underlining it in his script.

In exploring the "craft" of comedy as well as the "art" or comic principles of the genre, improv can be used either as something freestanding, a performance responsible only to itself, or as part of the rehearsal process and therefore in service of the play at hand. Underscoring the uses of improv techniques is our firm belief that the best actors, whether in comedy or tragedy, are the most *playful* actors, and by that we mean actors willing to take outrageous risks, eager to embrace bizarre, ridiculous, and nonsensical circumstances, and to believe in them 100 percent.

Improv makes you think on your feet, a skill the actor will need to use onstage no matter how carefully he has rehearsed. Something might go wrong: an actor not coming in on cue—this never happens, right?—or forgetting his line or jumping a whole page in the script. But, we are not just talking about accidents. If it is true that no two performances are exactly the same, just as no two audiences are— there is usually a different mood and hence a different reaction in the Saturday matinee audience from the audience who comes to see the show that evening—by thinking on your feet, you will be able to adjust to these nuances. And, what is more, you will be able to find new dimensions to your character, new ways and variations in enacting him over the course of a run. Most actors will admit their performance improves during this time. Being on your toes allows you to give a good performance and to be prepared as that performance evolves from opening night to the last show.

Our point is that practicing improv is useful to good comic acting because it works all the muscles, physical and psychological, that an actor needs trained. It prepares you to fight against multiple and varied obstacles, to become comfortable creating different tactics, and to believe in a series of outrageous given circumstances. An actor on script only works one set of "givens" per show, whereas an improv actor works with multiple obstacles every night.

The "paradox" of improv is that, when it works, when it is done well, it looks scripted, rehearsed, and the pleasure the audience takes— whether fellow actors onstage or an audience in the house—is that they know you and your fellow actors are also functioning in the moment. Oh sure, do enough improv and you build up a bank account of lines, physical shtick, and responses. Work long enough with your company and you can often predict where they are going in the skit, or what they need from you. With experience doing it, improv becomes a little less spontaneous. Still, it is happening on the spot, and you're on the spot as well. It's like riding a bucking bronco: you are generally good for a minute or so, but the skill is in going longer—without falling off.

For the comedic actor, improv complements the liveliness of scripted comedy. You've really got to be alert to everything happening. Simultaneously, you are taking risks and thereby trusting your imagination, but these are risks that must fit in with whatever your fellow improv partners are doing. If you create an improv character who has some traits in common with the character you'll be playing before an audience, you just might find surprising and compelling moments for that character in the scripted comedy.

When rehearsing your comic scripted character, you have to watch and listen very carefully to the events around you in order to connect with your fellow actors, to respond to them truthfully. Coming up with funny material on the spot underscores the same urgency the scripted comic character has to feel in satisfying a need, thinking of compelling and surprising tactics to overcome whatever obstacles are in his way. The pursuit of a need against obstacles is the action of your character. This is why improv reinforces the idea that acting is mainly a reaction to an action, not merely a passive expression of a feeling or emotion.

Valuable in itself, as well as during the rehearsal process, improv can even help the actor during a run of the show by increasing his ability to imbue scripted comedy with the illusion of the first time. Small details of a performance vary from night to night, and so improv keeps actors from being bound by that ideal performance they thought they had developed in rehearsal. It forces them to let go of preconceived outcomes in favor of a dynamic series of events that are ostensibly happening right now.

You depend on your fellow actors in a comedy. What they do onstage affects what you do, whether they miss a line or give an especially fine performance that enhances your own. Actors *feed* one another. Again, improv takes this notion to the extreme because it teaches complicity— the absolute need to work with others, to support them, to give as well as take.

Improv—in which you become one of the playwrights—gives you a special perspective on what the comedy's actual playwright has done, has given you. Improv can increase your understanding of how to create a beginning–middle–end structure for the arc of the character as it progresses through these various structural phases. Improv, particularly long-form improv, requires the actor to understand exposition (the "who"/"what"/"when"/"where" of a scene), rising action/conflict, and the need for resolution, which are the underlying structures of scripted scenes.

Short-Form Improvisations

We have found the following games and exercises to be particularly beneficial, offering well-known techniques that comedy actors can use to sharpen their skills. Drawing on our own experience with these improvs, many of which have been suggested by other commentators, we have grouped them according to six overarching elements of comic acting.[1]

Warm-Ups, Relaxation, Focus

Needless to say, improvisational work requires a flexible, tension-free body, and so warming up becomes absolutely essential. Each of the following stretches and exercises are designed to help you achieve a loose, relaxed, and focused physical and mental state.

Body and Mind

We like to do this two-part exercise after stretching to relax the body and mind.

Part One: Lie on the floor, feet and knees flat on the ground, with your hands by your sides, palms upward. First, isolate your feet and flex the muscles, then hold that flex for ten seconds. Try your best to keep the calves relaxed, and only flex the muscles in your feet. Next, isolate the calf muscles, keeping the muscles in your feet and upper legs relaxed. Hold for ten seconds. Then, flex the thighs, keeping the calves and hips relaxed. Repeat these isolations with the hips and buttocks, the abdominals, the chest, the shoulders, the neck, and finally the face. Once you have worked all of these areas, do an entire body flex, from the toes to the face. Hold this flex for as long as you can. When you end the flex, all the muscles in your body should feel relaxed and tension free.

Part Two: Breathe deep and long, in through the nose, out through the mouth. As you breathe in, imagine that the air that you breathe in is blue, and the carbon dioxide that you breathe out is red. See these colors in your mind's eye, and continue this for five minutes.

Now, breathing in and out in long, slow breaths, imagine that you are in the place that makes you feel the most comfortable, the most secure, the happiest. Look around at this place. It could be your grandmother's living room or on the grass by a lake—anywhere you like, but it should be the place that makes you feel the safest, and the most relaxed. Use your imagination to smell the scents, feel the textures, see the colors. If it's outside, feel the sun on your skin, the breeze in your hair. If it's indoors, notice the quality of light and the temperature of the room, and so on, engaging all of your senses. Continue to breathe long and slow breaths, and let this place fill you with serenity. Let all the tension, fears, and frustrations of your day-to-day life fall away. Stay in this place for five to ten minutes, letting everything that's negative in your life be replaced by positivity, the feeling that you are safe and secure. When you feel that all the tension has gone from your body and mind, slowly roll to the right and stand. Now you are ready to work.

Countdown

After this relaxation exercise, it is often necessary to put energy back into the body and voice. One way to do this is through a game we call "Countdown." Starting with the right hand, shake it as hard as you can without hurting yourself, while counting 1, 2, 3, 4, 5, 6, 7. Then repeat, as fast and loudly as you can with the left hand, followed by the right foot and then the left foot. Then repeat, counting only to 6 with the right and left hands and feet. Then count to 5, and so on down to 1. If you do this in a group, everyone should feed off everyone else's vocal and physical energy, moving and speaking together as a group.

Whoosh

"Whoosh" is another game designed as a warm-up to get the energy flowing. Participants stand in a circle, and one person starts by clapping both hands together, turning to the left or right and shouting "whoosh." Let the whoosh go around the circle; then, after that, anyone can shout "whoosh" and continue around the circle, or throw both hands in the air and shout "whoa." That "whoa" stops the flow in one direction and sends it in the opposite direction. The next person can either say "whoosh" and continue the flow in one direction or "whoa" it back in the other. After this, someone can point to anyone in the circle and shout "zap." That person has a choice: they can continue the "whoosh" in either direction, or they can "zap" it back to any other person. We like to raise the stakes by putting anyone who makes a mistake into the center of the circle, until there are only two players left. Those two players are the winners.

Listening, Staying Connected

Actors are dependent on one another to create dialogue growing out of a specific given situation, and improv teaches them to listen to their fellow actors and engage in real communication together. Unlike doing a character in a scripted play, in improv you *can't get by* doing only your own part; if you're not listening and responding to what is being said to you, the scene won't make sense. You've got to collaborate with your improv partner — "feed him with a spoon," as one director describes it. Even in a scripted play, if you try to get by on your own, you won't succeed, as the success of the performance depends on actors listening to and connecting with others. Improv can help in learning how to be totally absorbed with what is happening right now with the person onstage with you; it will keep you focused on the moment, not on what has gone before or what may happen next. This can increase your ability to imbue scripted comedy with a freshness, a sense of the present, as if what is happening onstage on this particular night of performance has never happened before — this, despite the audience's knowing they are seeing the play midway during the run.

Pick-Up Story

This game requires excellent listening skills, and involves a number of people standing in a line. An actor or director points at someone and that person must begin telling a story. It can be about anything, but the more outlandish the better. When chosen, the person must continue speaking until the director points to another person. That person picks up exactly where the last one left off. If chosen, you must make the effort to keep the ball rolling, not trying to be clever but saying the first thing that comes to mind. The story has to make narrative sense, but the elements can be as fantastic and outlandish as the imagination will allow.

One Word at a Time

This game takes "Pick-up Story" to the next level. The director or audience requires a theme to which the story must generally adhere. The actors again stand in a line, but instead of telling large chunks of the story, the actors are only allowed to speak one word at a time. This is best done sequentially down the line, so each actor knows when their turn will be. They have to listen carefully and wait for their turn to speak. However, there can be no planning ahead, as each actor is bound by the specific thing that the person before them chooses to say.

"Yes … and" Line

"Yes … and" exercises help to keep the actor thinking and reacting in the moment, and not be locked in by whatever they may have developed in rehearsal. These exercises force the actor to listen very carefully to what is being said and observe what is being done, which helps him to let go of preconceived outcomes in favor of a dynamic series of events that are ostensibly happening right now. In " 'Yes … and' line," actors form two lines (A and B) vertically on the stage — three to five people stacked 10 feet apart. The two most upstage should approach each other and sit on a bench. Lines alternate with regard to who is the first one to speak. The speaker should make a statement, about anything — the more bizarre and specific, the better. The second person should accept this offering and add to it somehow. The two should keep talking until they hear "switch." They then move to the back of the line, and two new speakers from lines A and B respectively take their place on the bench. Those returning to the back of the line should choose new partners so that there is as much variation as possible the next time that initial actor from line A takes the bench.

Sound and Movement

The actors form a circle. One person starts by making a sound and a physical gesture. The person to the immediate left must mimic exactly what the first actor said (and how she said it) and what she did. Natural changes will occur as the sound/movement goes around the circle, but the point is to listen and watch carefully so as to be able to recreate exactly what you were given.

Building Characters

One of the greatest benefits of improv is that it requires you to create and develop many different characters, and it's important in both improv and scripted comedy to create characters that are internally and externally real and fully fleshed out. Clearly, scripted drama requires the actor to understand the physical, psychological, and emotional traits of a character. In fact, so does improv. The more specific you can make your character, the more effective the improvisation. Specificity lends truth and believability to any scene, and that includes external information like energy level, vocal rhythm and tempo, vocal quality, and appearance, as well as internal information such as moral standards and attitudes, ambitions, fears, dreams, inhibitions, complexes, and so on. The more information the actor can provide about the character, the more real and therefore more interesting the scene will be. The following improvs can help the actor to understand the importance of specificity to character.

Changing Bodies

This exercise offers actors a chance to experiment with alternate physical states. First, the group walks at a medium pace about the room. Walk in the way you normally would. At some point, the director/ instructor calls out various conditions or professions that differ from those in the group. For example,

"Walk like a 10-year-old child."
"Walk like a 90-year-old adult."
"Walk like a ballerina."
"Walk like body-builder."
"Walk like a politician."
"Walk like a soldier."
"Walk like a beauty pageant queen."
"Walk like a high-school bully."
"Walk like a long-distance runner."
"Walk like a professional wrestler."

The actors should pay attention to the way their entire body changes with each suggestion. What part of their body do they lead with (e.g., chin, chest, forehead, pelvis)? How does the tension in certain parts of the body change? Pay attention to the way the feet come into contact with the ground. Is it a heavy or light step? Is it bouncy or plodding? How does the rhythm or tempo of the body moving through space change?

Rapid-Fire Interrogation

One actor stands in the middle of a circle of other actors. One by one, the actors in the circle bombard the person in the center with questions about a character they've created. The actor in the center must turn to each questioner and attempt to answer their question in as much detail as possible. As the questions mount in quick succession, the person in the middle will often become flustered and confused. The challenge is to answer as many questions as possible before this happens.

No Admittance

This game clarifies and amplifies character. One person is seated onstage and another enters, trying to gain admittance to an unspecified location. The seated person must take on the traits of the entering person, amplifying his dominant characteristics and mirroring them back to the person trying to gain admittance. The person trying to enter takes what he is being given and heightens it as well. Finally, after being denied entrance, he exits and then enters again as another character, with different traits.

Character Mirrors

The actors stand in a circle. Each player has a character that they've thought of (or one that belongs to a scripted play), and a caller asks them a question. For example, "What is the worst thing that you've ever done?" "What is the most embarrassing moment of your life?" "What was your childhood like?" That player must then answer the question in as vivid a manner as possible. The other players then mimic his or her words, voice, gestures, mannerisms, and so on. The caller then indicates another player and that player continues the story, using the same characteristics as the first.

Building Characters

One of the best exercises for practicing both internal and external character building, this game forces the actor to make rapid-fire choices based on the suggestions about a character's makeup that three players generate. First, three actors take the stage. The first actor says the character's first name. The second actor provides the middle name; the third actor, the character's last name. Then, the first actor briefly describes one of the character's attributes: "He is a depressed person with a limp." The next two actors must also create a descriptive phrase about the character; for example, "He constantly talks to himself" and "He lives with his mother." Then, each of the actors creates their own physicalization of the character and they all exit the stage.

Conflict

In the late nineteenth century, the French writer and critic Ferdinand Brunetière claimed that the most important component of drama—and we're paraphrasing here slightly—was a man in conflict with the external forces surrounding him.[2] Nowadays, it's pretty much a universally accepted fact that comedy needs conflict to get and hold an audience's attention. Frankly, happy, contented people onstage are boring to watch. What pulls us in is conflict. The underlying structure of almost all plays, movies, and television shows is,

1. a person or persons want something very badly;
2. obstacles arise, in various forms (other people, natural forces, society, fate, etc.); and

3. that person, protagonist, or antagonist must think of tactics to overcome those obstacles.

The result—conflict. We stay in our seat in the theatre for two or more hours because we want to see whether that character will be successful in overcoming those obstacles. In comedy, they usually are. In tragedy, they often are not. We always tell our actors that they have to fight to win (by creating varied and compelling tactics) and never to give up trying to satisfy their character's needs. Fighting to win and continuing to do so, never giving up—these are the wellsprings of action taken by the comic character.

Improv emphasizes action over emotions. Since it involves two or more actors working off a situation, an event in which they are caught up—two strangers stuck in an elevator, a noisy neighbor bursting into a domestic argument—improv reinforces the idea that acting is, first and foremost, a reaction in response to an action, not merely an expression of a feeling or emotion. Any display of feelings or emotions has to be rooted in action. Even the comic monologue depends on the character's reacting to something—his treatment at the hands of a pushy mother-in-law, the perils of working for a lecherous boss. Improv teaches us to be specific with our imagination, to duplicate in an unrehearsed way a given situation and the concomitant reaction to it a playwright would use to translate her general concept of a character into something seen and heard onstage. The following exercises are designed as practice in striving against opposing forces, and trying your utmost to win.

Conflict Improv

Here, the object is to build a scene around an issue of conflict between two people and then find a way to end the scene, to put a button on it. The director/instructor should choose a "who"/"what"/"when"/"where," or the audience can choose it. Here are some sample situations that call out for a resolution, an ending:

restaurant—waiter and disgruntled diner

restaurant—coat check attendant and customer whose coat is lost

home—sisters want the house for the weekend

home—sisters want the car for Friday night

apartment—neighbor having a party, one neighbor needs to sleep

apartment—the parents of two children who got in a fight

Neither actor should quit fighting or concede victory to the other.

Push My Button

In this game, the actors build a scene around a simple petty argument between a couple, creating a beginning, middle, and end. The beginning establishes context: who, what, where. The middle is where one person brings up a petty annoyance that expands into a full-blown argument. Let it be something the character says that ignites the argument. Milk the argument for all the humor it has. Then find a way to end the scene. Take three minutes and plan out its beginning, middle, and end. Situations might include an armed homeowner meeting a burglar; a homeowner and a repair person who has taken far too long and too many liberties; a fan who has won dinner and drinks with a famous person; friends camping in scary woods; two people in a jail cell where one has been there ten years, the other just arrived today; a boss firing a long-term employee; extras on a film set; or ex-lovers meeting after five years.

Mutually Exclusive Objectives

The object of this game is to block the objectives of your partner. Two actors begin the game with two mutually exclusive goals (given to them by the director/instructor privately); for example, one actor is a sibling who wants the family car to go on a date with someone they've been in love with for a long time, and they have finally convinced that person to go out with them (keep the stakes high), while the other actor wants the car to take friends to a concert of a favorite band. They cannot both get what they want, so they must use every tactic they can think of (short of physical violence) to try and do so. Neither actor should quit or concede victory to the other.

Status

The late, great theatre artist Keith Johnstone made a significant contribution to acting and improv theory when he introduced the concept of "status" to its lexicon. The idea of using status as a defense against and a tool with which to manipulate the world was so simple and yet so important in creating and developing characters that it caused a quiet revolution in acting theory. In his seminal book *Impro: Improvisation and the Theatre*, Johnstone observed a basic fact about human nature, as follows:

> Once you understand that every sound and posture implies a status, then you perceive the world quite differently, and the change is probably permanent. In my view, really accomplished actors, directors, and playwrights are people with an intuitive understanding of the status transactions that govern human relationships ... I'd suggest that a good play is one that ingeniously displays and reverses the status between characters.[3]

According to Johnstone, everyone has a preferred status, be it high or low (or some gradation between the two), and in everyday social interactions we try to manipulate situations so that we can maneuver ourselves into that preferred position. Status improv can help you to use the concept to create complex, believable characters, and to achieve your objectives with other characters.

Status Wander

This exercise introduces some of the basic elements of status work. The people are separated into two groups: A and B. Both groups walk at a medium pace throughout the room, making eye contact with those they encounter. During this stroll, the instructions for the A group are that they must make and hold eye contact with those they pass. They should not break eye contact until that person has passed them. The B group must make eye contact with those they pass, but then immediately look away. Look, make eye contact, look away; look, look away. Once the group has done this for three to five minutes, they stop and discuss how individuals from both groups made them feel about the other group's people and about themselves. Chances are the As made the Bs feel small, weak, while the Bs made the As feel as if the Bs were weak, lacking confidence, or—worse—sneaky and devious. The Bs more likely than not made the As feel strong, powerful, and in control while, to the Bs, the As seemed arrogant, haughty, and disapproving of them. Now switch— the As becoming Bs, and vice versa—repeating the exercise for the same amount of time, with the discussion to follow.

Status Conversation

This exercise explores status even further. Form pairs and decide which person will be partner A and which partner B. You are going to have a conversation about any topic: the weather, politics—anything. Partner A again will make steady eye contact, not looking away. She will hold her head steady, not moving it all, no nodding in acknowledgment, no turning away, or looking up or down. A will also pepper her sentences with lengthy, extended "uhs," "ums," and "ahs," or just generally elongate the vowels in her words. This is stereotypical high-status behavior; consider the character Lumbergh from the movie *Office Space*, whose signature line is "Um, I'm gonna need you to go ahead and come in on Saturday." Meanwhile, partner B should make eye contact, but then quickly look away. Look, look away. He should fidget and exhibit nervous behavior, touching his face and hair frequently. Like partner A, he should pepper his sentences with "uhs," "ums," and "ahs," but they should be short, not elongated like partner As. This is stereotypical low-status behavior. After conversing for three to five minutes, the partners should switch: A becomes B, and B becomes A. When both partners have been both A and B, they should discuss how they felt being an A and a B, and how their partner made them feel as an A and as a B.

Highest/Lowest

Create a scene with a specific location, in which the actors play characters at divergent ends of the social scale—a king and a beggar, an aggressive woman and a timid man, the star of a show and someone from the stage crew, a liberal intellectual from New York and a Tea Party Republican from Kansas. Then switch roles. Perhaps even have the character on the "lowest" rung somehow get the better of the "highest" one by showing him up, exposing a flaw, or hitting him with some news that knocks him off a pedestal.

The Game

One aspect of long-form improv that has proved to be beneficial to scripted comedy is the concept of "the game." Successful improv depends on a performer's ability to recognize and play "the game" of the moment to his utmost. So, what is the game? It is that first unusual element, an unexpected thing that breaks from predictable patterns of normalcy in the events, circumstances, or behavior of the scene. For the comedic actor, the ability to see, understand, and play the game that is happening onstage in front of him is the key to successful improvisation, and is also excellent practice for textual comedic roles. In improv, the performer must *find* the game, while in textual theatre the game is provided by the playwright. The seventeenth-century French dramatist Molière was a master of the game. For example, in *Tartuffe*, when Orgon first enters into his home, he continually asks about and sympathizes with Tartuffe, while the maid keeps replying how sick Orgon's wife is:

> **Orgon** [...] What has happened here? How do they all do?
> **Dorine** My lady the day before yesterday had a fever all day, and
> was sadly out of order with a strange headache.
> **Orgon** And Tartuffe?
> **Dorine** Tartuffe? Extremely well, fat, fair, and fresh-coloured.
> **Orgon** Poor man!
> **Dorine** At night she had no stomach, and could not touch a bit of
> supper, the pain in her head continued so violent.
> **Orgon** And Tartuffe?
> **Dorine** He supped by himself before her, and very heartily ate half a
> brace of partridge, and half leg of mutton hashed.
> **Orgon** Poor man![4]
>
> (Act One, Scene Four)

Orgon's total disinterest in his own wife coupled with his misplaced concern with Tartuffe is the game provided by Molière. For improvisers, finding the game is all about discovering an anomaly, identifying a break with decorum, and then developing it and locking it down into a pattern that, if followed, will bring about big laughs from an audience. As noted in The Upright Citizens Brigade's *Comedy Improvisation Manual*,

> Repeatedly answering the question "If this unusual thing [the prem-
> ise of the game] is true, then what else is true?" creates a comic pat-
> tern. Each answer to this question (or similar, related versions of this
> question) is called a "Game move." A combination of game moves
> forms a pattern that we call a "Game."[5]

Analyzing the Game

This exercise is designed to help actors identify and describe the game. Two actors take the stage and begin a scene by establishing a clear "who"/"what"/"when"/"where." Other actors observe and pay careful attention in order to notice the first unusual thing that occurs. When someone spots that unusual thing, they raise their hand and comment on why they think it was an example of the game. The group then discusses the event and suggests ways to continue working off it. The improvisers then continue the scene, with the goal of embellishing and amplifying the game.

Patterns

This exercise is for four people—two onstage and two offstage—sitting to the side. The two people onstage perform a scene with a clear "who"/"what"/"when"/"where," while the two offstage watch and look for a pattern to emerge, which is usually the first thing that causes a big laugh from the audience. When that first laugh occurs, the two people offstage tag out the two players and begin a whole new scene, though maintaining the pattern they've observed. Their goal is to embellish and amplify the pattern. They assume two different characters involved in a different situation, but keep what was humorous about the first situation as the basis for the new scene. For example, if the first scene was about a lumberjack who is too afraid to cut down a tree, the second scene might be about a surgeon too afraid to operate on a patient.

Repetition

Working off a suggestion from the audience, two actors begin an improvised scene and seek to establish a "who"/"what"/"when"/ "where." When one of the players thinks that the first unusual thing has occurred, they should repeat the specific line that made up that unusual thing, but not in character. They should step out of character and merely repeat verbatim what their partner said, and then repeat it again. The partner who originally said the line should then repeat it one more time, word for word—the line should be spoken at least four to five times. Now that the line constituting the first unusual thing has been repeated and firmly established, the players should resume the scene with the goal of creating and amplifying a pattern. This pattern thus becomes the game. Both partners are responsible for contributing to the pattern of the game.

Improv and the Comic Actor

Improv and acting exercises teach actors to focus, listen, and be in the present on stage, giving them another tool with which to develop their character and keep their performance fresh. As we have seen, improv can comprise everything from short form to long form ("the game"), as well as simultaneously run parallel to but differ from scripted comedy. Doing improv well can even conceal, for a time, the fact that it is spontaneous—a play without a script or any rehearsal. It can prepare the actor physically as well as mentally, through warm-up and relaxation, sharpening his take on the character he is to play while also staying connected when in dialogue with other characters. Like laughter itself, improv involves both the body and the brain.

* * *

In the next chapter, we move from the actor's preparation for a play, whether such preparation takes place at rehearsals or during the run itself, to those aspects of playing a comic character that an actor will want to consider as he fashions a role. We call them "rules," though there is surely nothing absolute about them, for each will be shaped by the occasion, the special nature, and hence the demands of a particular comedy. Accordingly, we look at devising a character analysis and history, playing those obstacles at the heart of the comic character, attending to clarity of expression and awareness of the body, mastering joke structure and comic timing, negotiating between making your character "too real" and "not real enough," and putting something of yourself or your life experiences into the comic character. Employing a similar analytical approach to that used in Chapter 1 in relation to laughter, we illustrate these topics by applying them to characters in Moira Buffini's black comedy, *Dinner*. How do they relate not only to the character (his or her motivation, inner nature, and subtext), but also to the actor who crafts that character?

Notes

1   There are a number of useful books on the subject of improv. These
    include Viola Spolin, *Improvisation for the Theater: A Handbook of
    Teaching and Directing Techniques* (Evanston, IL: Northwestern
    University Press, 1963); Paul Ryan, *The Art of Comedy: Getting
    Serious about Being Funny* (New York: Back Stage Books, 2007);
    John Abbott, *The Improvisation Book: How to Conduct Successful
    Improvisation Sessions* (London: Nick Hern, 2007); Gavin Levy, *112
    Acting Games: A Comprehensive Workbook of Theatre Games for
    Developing Acting Skills* (Colorado Springs: Meriwether Publishing,
    2005); Gavin Levy, *275 Acting Games, Connected: A Comprehensive
    Workbook of Theatre Games for Developing Acting Skills* (Colorado
    Springs: Meriwether Publishing, 2010); Nancy Hurley, *175 Theatre
    Games: Warm-Up Exercises for Actors* (Colorado Springs: Meriwether
    Publishing, 2009); John Wright, *Why Is That So Funny?: A Practical
    Exploration of Physical Comedy* (New York: Limelight Editions, 2006);
    Tom Salinsky and Deborah Frances-White, *The Improv Handbook*:
    The Ultimate Guide to Improvising in Comedy, Theatre, and Beyond
    (New York: Continuum, 2008); Keith Johnstone, *Impro: Improvisation
    and the Theatre* (New York: Routledge/Theatre Arts Books, 1979);
    Dan Diggles, *Improv for Actors* (New York: Allworth Press, 2004); Brie
    Jones, *Improve with Improv!: A Guide to Improvisation and Character
    Development* (Colorado Springs: Meriwether Publishing, 1993).
2   Ferdinand Brunetière, "The Law of the Drama," trans. Philip M. Hayden,
    in *European Theories of the Drama: An Anthology of Dramatic Theory
    and Criticism from Aristotle to the Present Day*, ed. Barrett H. Clark
    (Cincinnati, OH: Stewart & Kidd, 1918), 404–14.
3   Johnstone, *Impro*, 72.
4   Molière, *Tartuffe*, trans. Henry Baker and James Miller, Dover Thrift Edition,
    ed. John Berseth (New York: Dover Publications, 2000), 6.
5   Matt Besser, Ian Roberts, and Matt Walsh, *The Upright Citizens Brigade
    Comedy Improvisation Manual* (New York: Council Comedy of Nicea, LLC,
    2013), 64.

3
BASIC RULES FOR THE COMIC ACTOR

Character Analysis and History

To bring a character to life, the actor has to determine what motivates him—the character's specific needs and wants. These should be borne in mind at every moment, as well as *why* the character wants what he wants, even though the character himself might not know.

Indeed, it is important for comic actors to consider a variety of questions surrounding that character's overall circumstances. After all, someone living in a fifty-room mansion is going to see and move through the world in a different way than someone brought up in a mobile home park by the highway. Therefore, backstory is often key to the creation of complex, multidimensional characters. The first question the actor John A. Ferraro asked himself when preparing for a role was, "Do characters in plays exist before the curtains come up?"—a question that "fascinated" him and one to which he always gave a positive answer.[1]

So, to create a comprehensive backstory, actors should ask themselves these questions about their characters—and the more specific choices made, the better:

"Who am I?"
"What do I want?"
"What stands in my way?"
"Why must I have it now?"
"What am I willing to do to get it?"
"What time is it? Which day of the week?"

"What time of year is it?"
"Which year is it?"
"Where am I?"
"What are my relationships?"
"What do I say about myself?"
"What do other characters say about me?"
"What does the playwright say about me?"
"What do the stage directions say about me?"

Some of your answers may be adjusted, even contradicted, by facts emerging later in the play. No problem—you can always make changes. Some questions often elicit a general consensus among cast members or those reading the scene for the first time, but there are no "right" or absolute answers. Each actor fashions the character and, to do this, draws from personal experiences and her interpretation of the text.

Character Interview

This exercise is especially helpful in the early stages of rehearsal. Each actor has a turn in front of the rest of the cast and the directing team. Anyone in the group can ask any question they like about the character: his background, his likes and dislikes, typical ways of dealing with everyday events including physical and verbal expressions, and so on. Nothing is off limits as regards the character's overall physical, emotional, psychological, and social makeup. So, for example,

"What makes you happy?"
"What is your greatest fear?"
"How do you think people perceive you?"
"What have you done in your life that you are most proud of?"
"How do you typically start your day?"
"What type of person are you attracted to? Repelled by?"
"What are your most cherished beliefs?"
"Are you religious? How religious? Which religion?"
"What makes you laugh?"
"Do you have a secret that you've never told anyone?"
"What cheers you up?"
"What embarrasses you?"

Note that the choice the actor makes in the moment as he responds to the question is not necessarily binding. After more extensive inquiry and based on information acquired later, he may feel that some of his answers were not grounded. But the value is that the actor starts to make choices about his character at an early stage of rehearsal and will remain critical about these choices from that point on.

Playing Obstacles

If an actor approaches a character superficially, through ungrounded or unmotivated physical shtick, he creates a caricature rather than a character, because the internal motivation is missing. Unless the audience understands the needs and desires of the character, their behavior will seem empty or unmotivated, and therefore confusing and not funny.

It's important to be funny without trying too hard, and the best way to do that is to establish the character's circumstances. Ask yourself questions about the character's life outside of the play, as if they existed in the real world and the play itself were just a specific time period in that life.

In "Grandeur without Pomp," François-Joseph Talma, one of the leading actors of his generation, pushed for the actor's identification with his or her character.[2] His "Reflections on Acting" (1825)[3] was so influential that the great director and theatre theorist Konstantin Stanislavski, by his own admission, would later incorporate it into his writings. For Talma, the actor should feel what the character feels, think what he thinks, and take an emotional journey like that of the onstage persona. Especially in comedy, Talma asserted, actors should use the stuff of their own personalities, their own experience, because they are portraying "real" people. In contrast, the actor of tragedy, portraying gods, royalty, and celebrated heroes, must find the character essentially in the text rather than real life.

To participate in Talma's "emotional journey," you should first find your character's inner self, and then weave it into the personality the character exhibits within the play. The more "truthful" your character, the more likely the audience will make connections between what you portray onstage and their own lives and the humor there.

Knowing the character's needs and desires is at one with the truth of the situation, and the word that embraces this concept is "obstacles." Comic characters focus on, struggle with, and will go to any lengths, no matter how extreme, to overcome obstacles: anything—human or not—standing in their way, threatening what they see as necessary to their happiness, self-fulfillment, success, or safety. If whatever they overcome allows them to fulfill their needs or desires, especially if they appear more ridiculous in doing so, the audience will find it funny, particularly if the obstacle is, from their perspective, self-inflicted.

Obstacles, of course, are not unique to comic characters. Hamlet, after all, struggles with his father's otherwise simple charge to kill his uncle and leave his mother's soul to heaven. If he were the average Elizabethan avenger, there would be no problem, no obstacle, but Hamlet, we know, thinks too much and needs to put action within a context—metaphysical, ethical, or existential. His obstacles are therefore self-inflicted, but he is the better for that since he is the only Renaissance revenger for whom we care.

Unlike Hamlet, however, comic characters overcome difficulties that are more basic, physical, practical, everyday; their needs are mundane, not philosophical.

Lost Object

This is a useful exercise for heightening an actor's struggle with an obstacle. The actor, performing as his character, engages in an improvisational struggle to find a lost object that has huge emotional significance for him. The actor thus has to think of an object that, if lost, would devastate him, and then create an amplified emotional response to find it, no matter what. If the actor imbues the object with enough importance, it will consume his attention and actions. The actor must commit 100 percent to the imaginary circumstances though, for if the lost object has little emotional weight, then the struggle will always be less than real, and the exercise will have diminished effectiveness. But if the actor chooses the object well, and commits himself totally to finding it, then every minute will generate more and more emotional effect. The exercise should last no more than fifteen minutes, and works best if the actor has lots of props. The director should add further obstacles by sending other characters from the play to distract the main actor from achieving his goal of finding the precious object.

Clarity of Expression

Comedy depends on its precision, its crispness. Drama can sometimes get away with being mumbled and messy, or even praised for being "so real." Realistic drama can often degenerate to a parody of Method acting, the delivery running from distinct to indistinct.

There is usually little such mumbling or incoherence in comedy, though. Even in David Ives's piece *Words, Words, Words*, in which all the characters are chimpanzees, the sounds made by the animals must be as clear and understandable as if they were delivering Noel Coward's crisp, witty, upper-class dialogue.

Such clarity of expression is at length inseparable from the speaking "style" of your character. You will want to ask yourself where she comes from, her social class, how the character's way of talking, her pronunciation, is influenced by circumstances—happy, sad, frustrating, unexpected. Does her vocabulary change, even slightly, as she gets excited trying to overcome an obstacle, as she nears achieving her desire? Does she adjust—again, ever so slightly—her speaking style with different characters in the play? What is the gap, if any, between her public (or social) voice and those moments when she is by herself, as in an aside or monologue, or in dialogue with someone she trusts? Words—the ones we use, how we deliver them, our attitude toward them, our style—are a mirror to the character, both as she interacts with others and in that interior "dialogue" only she can hear, with the latter at one with the subtext devised by the actor.

Alliteration Repetition

This improv technique, inspired by an exercise featured in Paul Ryan's book *The Art of Comedy*,[4] is designed to improve clarity and vocal precision. In it, two strangers meet at a bus stop, an airport, or a train station. Two chairs are situated on the stage. One actor is seated, looking out at the traffic going by. The second actor enters from the side with a sense of urgency and a strong *need* to talk to the seated stranger. They introduce themselves and ask each other what they do for a living, each answering using an alliterative profession such as:

Better-Built Brassiere Buyer; Bippity Boppity Blues Bugler; Boston Bird Bath Builder; Cheddar Cheese Cracker Checker; Cuban Cuckoo Clock Collector; Determined, Desirable, Diligent Dentist; Dutch Donut Double Dunker; Lemon–Lime Lollipop Licker; Magnificent Malaysian Map Maker; Ridiculous Rhodesian Rattlesnake Wrangler; Ripe Red Raspberry Rancher; Sweet and Sour Sausage Stuffer; Taco and Tamale Taster; Tennessee Tic-Tac-Toe Tester; Tippity Tip Tap Toe Tapper; Victorian Viennese Violin Varnisher; Wacky, Wiry, Wonderful Winner; Walla Walla Window Washer.

They continue chatting, constantly repeating what the other person said, slightly changing it to make the conversation move forward, and keeping their responses brief and their sentences short. This exercise forces the actor to stay in the moment, and not think about what they're going to say next. He must be fully present and listening. While the alliterative job descriptions are silly, you must be serious in your work. Let the other actor's energy feed you and pump you up. Be affected by him.

Body Awareness

Know what kind of body you have, and use its comedic qualities. John Candy relied on his large girth to generate humor, and Don Knotts used his skinny frame to create Andy Griffith's bumbling, neurotic deputy Barney Fife. Jim Carrey's rubber face, its contortions, is often as vital to the laughter as his dialogue. Comedy that tends toward slapstick, especially, demands a supple, flexible body, as do many farces. For example, the second act of Frayn's *Noises Off* takes place with a minimum of dialogue, and our enjoyment of the scene depends on how the actors move about, almost bumping into each other, evading one another by doing pratfalls, turning pirouettes as each tries to avoid the mad rush of bodies behind the set.

As a general rule, then, the comedic actor should be able to use his body as a malleable tool, enabling him to display the human condition in its myriad manifestations: health, neuroses, obsessions, awkwardness, deformity. We are talking here about what is commonly called "physical comedy," in which the body, along with the dialogue, produces the laughs.

Late in his career, Stanislavski began to shift his focus from emotions and a character's inner life to physical actions, what a character actually *does* in the play and how those *actions* affect the emotions generated by the actor. Then, he maintained that the way for the actor to work on a character was from the outside in, rather than from the inside out. Correct, clear physical actions give rise to truthful emotions and feelings inside the character. Stanislavski elaborated on this equation as follows:

> We artists must realize the truth that even small physical movements, when injected into "given circumstances," acquire great significance through their influence on emotion … why do I lay such exceptional stress on this elementary method of affecting our feelings? If you tell an actor that his role is full of psychological action, tragic depths, he will immediately begin to contort himself, exaggerate his passion, "tear it to tatters," dig around in his soul and do violence to his feelings. But if you give him some simple physical problem to solve and wrap it up in interesting, affecting conditions, he will set about carrying it out without alarming himself or even thinking too deeply whether what he is doing will result in psychology, tragedy or drama.[5]

Reflection of Self

This exercise comes from Gavin Levy's book *275 Acting Games*,[6] and involves the actor's ability to recognize what it is about his physical self that makes him unique and separate from others. The actor should find a space for himself, away from others, and begin to perform basic actions like combing his hair, buttoning a shirt, or washing his face. He should imagine that, while he is doing this, he is watching himself in a huge mirror that covers the length of the wall. He should continue these actions while watching himself carefully in the imaginary mirror for up to five minutes. Next, he repeats these actions, only now as the character he is playing. He can concentrate solely on these actions or add more similarly quotidian ones. The point is to note the differences between how the character performs the actions and how the actor does them. Does he perform them faster, slower, more smoothly, or more erratically? Is the character more methodical or more chaotic, coordinated or clumsy? The actor must constantly visualize himself in the mirror and follow each move very carefully. This lets him see what sets him apart from other actors, his character from other characters. It reinforces the actor's and the character's humanity, and it is this humanity that audiences respond to and connect with. Fat or skinny, short or tall, this exercise brings to light what the actor has to offer as a unique human being, and it's that realization that is the basis of a rapport with an audience.

Joke Structure/Comedic Timing

Telling a joke successfully onstage requires a certain amount of knowledge about what kind of joke it is and how it works. There are many different types of jokes—malapropisms, spoonerisms, overstatements, understatements, puns, double entendres—and each has its own unique method of delivery.

In *Play Production*, playwright/director Henning Nelms maintained that "laugh-getting depends 75 percent on the actor's technique and only 25 percent on the point of the joke."[7] In the book's chapter on comedy, Nelms systematized his own technique, laying out one of the most specific joke-delivery analyses ever published. He posited that it takes place in seven distinct stages. First, the "warning phrase" raises expectations, focusing attention on the actor, and presenting the incongruity at the basis of the comedy, in whole or in part. This is followed by the "warming phrase," a beat just before the comic line. The "punch" comes at the end of the joke—literally, at the end of the sentence—and is always short. One beat after that we get the "punch pause," or the time for the audience to react. Crucial to that reaction is the "snapper" with which the audience, laughing as a unit, their laughter growing, is given a laugh cue, such as a quick gesture or a snap of the finger. After another pause there comes "holding for the laugh," wherein the actors remain silent and motionless, and during which no important line can be spoken, although the gap can be filled with pantomime or stage business. Finally, we get "killing the laugh": after the audience's laughter has died away—and actors should kill the laugh as soon as it begins to weaken—the first words of the next speech are delivered emphatically; the audience, now knowing that "something important is coming," will become quiet and listen to the rest of the line. Nelms observed that, "If, instead of killing the laugh, a piece of comic business is inserted at this point, a new laugh will result."[8]

In *Since Stanislavski and Vakhtangov: The Method as a System for Today's Actor*, Lawrence Parke observed that the "comedy player ... has to build the comic character. Only occasionally can he simply clown his way through on his own unique talents to such a degree that he does not need anything else."[9] Though Parke was a Method traditionalist who spoke frequently of the inner life of the character, still he acknowledged the importance of joke timing, and the necessity for utilizing objective, external devices such as the "take":

> Timing of a comic variety will occur all by itself if the actor consistently *does takes* instead of jumping right back with dialogue or outgoing action of some kind. In fact, timing is not often the domain of the person who is speaking at the moment. It is the result of the next speaker's stopping to do a "take" (which may be amusing on its own).[10]

Whether as a stand-up comedian or a character delivering a joke embedded in a play's dialogue, the actor must also be aware of these stages (and their relationship) if the joke is to succeed. In *Directing Plays: A Working Professional's Method*, Stuart Vaughan offered his version of the stages previously suggested by Nelms: the plant (the clue needed for the audience to get the joke), the pause, the point (the solution to the joke, or the punch line), the amplifier (physical punctuation following the joke, and the space given to the audience to get the full extent of the joke), and the bridge (not part of the joke but the segue to the next one).[11]

Vaughan explored every aspect of joke-telling, analyzing in detail the rules and limitations of comedy acting, including those governing stage movement, timing, and issues of language. His position in the centuries-old argument over whether or not the comedic actor should attempt to identify with the thoughts and feelings of the character is clear: "I do not believe that 'what the actor feels' makes the slightest difference in the actor's playing or the audience's response to that playing, as long as the actor has prepared the role satisfactorily."[12]

Comedy's Fine Line: Too Real, Not Real Enough

To succeed in comedy, the actor must walk between naturalized and stylized behavior. Too natural and the actor will seem imprecise, unclear; the audience can become confused, the physical and verbal humor can be lost. If the actor scratches and mumbles his way through the scene, attempting to be someone who has just stepped unchanged out of real life, the jokes often do not work. Too stylized and the character's human qualities are lost and the performance seems superficial.

Conversely, if the actor is not natural enough he may run the risk of "face acting"—that is, acting in a superficial manner and relying on the face, or obvious gestures, to *show* the character's feelings and thoughts, rather than his embodying them in word and action. With face acting, the actor is creating a graphic but superficial relationship with the audience while he should be pursuing a relationship with the characters onstage based on needs and objectives. When the actor cares more about what the audience thinks than what the character thinks—not playing objectives and intentions, struggling with obstacles, or thinking of tactics to get what the character wants—he creates a disconnect between actors. Performing in a blatantly self-conscious way to get a laugh from the audience isolates your character from the others and the audience.

This disconnect can also happen during a run, especially after an actor has received a good response from the audience. The actor might tend to "play the comedy." Knowing what line or what facial expression or gesture gets the biggest laughs, the actor now wants nothing more than to recreate, if not top, yesterday's performance. He feels safe with what has worked so far, but this means, again, that he is trying to satisfy the wrong set of needs—his, as opposed to the character's.

In his article "Actors and Acting," the American actor Henry Irving spoke against "playing the comedy," emphasizing instead the need for an actor to identify psychologically and emotionally with his character: "If tears can be summoned at his will and subject to his control, it is true art to utilize such a power, and happy is the actor whose sensibility has at once such delicacy and discipline."[13] Years later, Maria Aitken, in *Style: Acting in High Comedy*, would make a similar argument regarding comic acting, affirming that the character's "emotions are as real and serious to him as any in tragedy: any attempt by the actor to dilute them 'because it's comedy' would be fatal."[14]

So the actor must, above all, forget about the audience, and forget about getting a laugh. Keeping focus on the character's needs, struggles, and obstacles, as well as—equally important—the character's relationships with others will enable the audience to see the process of communication among the characters. Onstage, five shallow stand-up comedians are as bad as one. The comic actor must constantly hear, react, process, and respond to the other characters onstage. If a character is speaking, it means that he wants something, and he should be urgently eager to get that something. Therefore, being understood and perceived correctly ought always to be important both to the character and to the actor. If not, the audience will deem the interaction false or shallow.

The important thing is that the sender and receiver are connecting: in playing the scene, it is vital that your response comes out of what you *perceive* the other is saying so the conversation will seem justified.

Yourself and Your Comic Character

When we talk about approaching a comic character from the inside as well as outside, we enter a world beyond the theatre as well as that implicit in the text. The playwright, setting down the character on the page, doubtless has his or her own answers to the questions. But theatre, after all, is a collaborative venture among playwright, director, actors, designers—and the audience. The only way of "scoring" your answers would be to consider whether they help you to identify with the character. Do they allow you to make that character funny in the human, psychological, and therefore meaningful way we have been talking about? Do your responses avoid making the character shallow, a stereotype? Do they flesh out a character that will resonate with the audience?

This relationship between one's self and the comic role you play is at the heart of the Method's focus on an actor's using "affective memory" or "emotional memory" to generate analogous states in the character. Yet, critics of the Method have long asserted that it is inappropriate for use in comedies, arguing that the actor may become overwhelmed by emotion while dredging up such highly charged memories and, therefore, unable to concentrate on the external elements of a comedic performance: language, joke delivery, timing—not to mention the other actors.

Our response to this concern is a qualified one: we think the actor should feel the character's emotion, but not indulge in it. Emotions in comedy (especially negative emotions such as fear, rage, or sadness) tend to be less intense and more mercurial than those in drama, and the actor often has less time to transition in and out of these emotional states. Comedy requires a slight detachment, an imperceptible "wink" to the audience that lets them know the actor is not in any "real" emotional pain. If the audience *does* perceive the character to be genuinely hurting, their empathic response may overcome their reaction to the humor, and nothing kills comedy like empathy. Further, if the actor places too much importance on producing and sustaining emotion, the performance will run the risk of looking self-indulgent as well as strange, since most people in real life try to hide their feelings instead of putting them on display.

Still, the question remains: Is "emotional memory" appropriate for comedy? Again, our answer is qualified: yes it is, as long as it is used by the actor to call up a specific need rather than a specific emotion, and one that is appropriately analogous to the character's own. The key is that this need must lead to an action that satisfies the needs of the character. "Playing the emotion" is as deadly as "playing the joke." In both cases, the actor is attempting to satisfy his own need (to affect the audience), rather than that of his character.

Most Method practitioners, from Stanislavski to Strasberg, have advocated simplicity, truth, and a connectedness between internal need and external necessity. Doug Moston underscores this collaboration in *Coming to Terms with Acting: An Instruction Glossary*: "Playing comedy means creating the proper inner life. Your *choice* will determine whether you're exploiting the comedic elements of the script or not."[15] For Moston, the choices the actor makes about the inner reality of the character are just as important as the external rules governing the comedy. Choose the wrong internal motivation—that is, make the wrong emotional choice for the character—and the humor could be lost. Using Neil Simon's *The Odd Couple* (1965) as an example, Moston contends that if the actor playing Oscar approaches the role with all hostility and no love toward Felix, the audience won't laugh. Instead, they will feel uncomfortable, empathetic toward Felix, and unsympathetic toward Oscar. According to Moston, actors should always look for the love, and therefore the vulnerability, in their characters. Vulnerability is what makes an audience connect with the character, and thus laugh at his foibles and missteps.

One of the most respected books about acting in contemporary comedy, and comedy in general, is Henri Szeps's *All in Good Timing*. Therein, in an analysis of the art of timing, defined as "knowing when the audience is ready for the next piece of information,"[16] Szeps synthesizes the conventions, the objective requirements of comic acting, with the subjective principles of the Method in stressing the importance of *living* the part, rather than merely *representing* it. In order to accomplish this, the book advances a technique very similar to emotion memory, the "loading up" of actual memories, which Szeps terms "references":

> References would not be necessary if we could keep believing in the story indefinitely, and if we were able to spontaneously feel what we were meant to feel at any moment in the play. But anyone who has even done amateur theatre will tell you that that does not happen … Now is the time when you will need the skills, the little thoughts, the sleight of hand to trick yourself.[17]

Moreover, he reasons that "if you are deliberately trying to show your feelings in real life, it is more than likely that you are either lying or mad."[18] So the problem for the comic actor is, first, to generate the feeling or emotion, and then to fight against it, as only then will the audience accept the character as a truthful representation of a human being.

Dinner

Some reviewers as well as audiences have seen Moira Buffini's *Dinner* as little more than a formula play.[19] Take five or six characters, all with needs, fetishes, neuroses, obstacles, and pasts that in some cases have intertwined, and then put them around a dining table and let them go at it. Perhaps bring in, halfway through the dinner, an uninvited surprise guest so that he or she can shake things up even more. So, if your character is a generic type, what do you do?

In *Dinner*, we have the hostess, Paige; cynical, a control freak, celebrating the publication of her husband Lars's latest book by serving a four-course meal that is her "art," a way of satirizing and exposing both Lars and her guests. There's Lars, who is about to divorce Paige, and is a pretentious guru whose self-help book *Beyond Belief* takes Ayn Rand to the extreme, predicting a "psychological apocalypse"[20] unless the individual finds his "psyche-drive."[21] Hal, a microbiologist, still guilt ridden over the suicide of his first wife, arrives sporting his new girlfriend, Siân, a self-styled "sex pot"[22] given to crude, at best bitter jokes. Then there's Wynne, who insists she's not a feminist but an "eroticist,"[23] dumped by her lover because she exhibited a surrealist painting of his genitals. Halfway through dinner, Mike enters, a blue-collar worker posing as a thief, hoping to absorb some of the culture of this group of "superficially successful but utterly dim-witted middle-class acquaintances."[24] Finally, there is the mostly silent waiter, who pops in and out, filling numerous drink orders from Paige, serving the various "stages" of her dinner, and who, in an ending worthy of a black comedy, turns out to be an assassin she's hired from an Internet ad.

How does the actor make his character something more than the generic dinner-table type? By looking at each of *Dinner*'s characters in terms of the seven approaches discussed in this chapter, we can see that a "rule" applied to one could just as easily be applied to all.

Character Analysis/History: Paige

Paige, of course, is the sum of both her dialogue and her actions throughout the play, and, no less, what the other characters say about her. But which aspects of her personality might the actor glean from the script?

She insists (too much so?) that she is "perfectly in control of the situation,"[25] although that control can also "crumble"—the word used in the stage direction when Lars challenges her to go through with her suicide.[26] Her imperious line to the Waiter at the start of the play—"Am I paying you to stand there?"—is immediately undercut with, "Yes, I think I am."[27] If one of her guests fails to arrive, if they "snub" her, then she threatens, "I'd kill myself,"[28] a hyperbole that will turn literally true at the end of the play.

Siân spots what drives Paige when she observes, "I think it's to do with control."[29] Paige suspects that her husband is going to file for divorce and so her humor at his expense may reflect her anxiety, as when she claims not to have read his new book, the reason for tonight's celebration.[30] One of the weapons she contributes to the game of naming instruments of death is a "traitor's kiss."[31] Is the traitor her husband?

On the surface, the lobsters are a means to test her guests—will they boil and eat them or let them live in "the ornamental pond out there on the patio"?[32] Still, her description of the main course seems self-referential: the lobster is "soft and naked beneath its defences, as helpless as mankind, awaiting its final fate."[33] Later she observes, "This lobster reminds me of me."[34]

Paige takes refuge in the ultimate demonstration of self-control. In her words, "To take control of one's death requires the kind of courage that few of us possess. To attempt and fail is a tragedy. One has to seek and embrace it with complete dedication."[35] This hostess whose witty dialogue is the benchmark for the play ends without words: for her, one must "embrace the silence that's to come" and thereby "say nothing."[36]

Now, with such "information" in mind, as selective as the citations above may be, how would the actor answer the questions we posed at the start of this chapter pertaining to character analysis/history:

"Who am I?"
"What do I want?"
"What stands in my way?"
"Why must I have it now?"
"What am I willing to do to get it?"
"What time is it? Which day of the week?"
"What time of year is it?"
"Which year is it?"
"Where am I?"
"What are my relationships?"

"What do I say about myself?"

"What do other characters say about me?"

"What does the playwright say about me?"

Each actor, of course, will have her own answers or speculations here, and those answers will in turn flesh out the character, surely making Paige more than a stereotype. In this way, the actor collaborates with the playwright.

Playing Obstacles: Lars

Lars's obstacle is crystal clear, and, like the self-publicizing pseudo-philosopher he is, he defines it for the other guests: he wants to overcome what he calls "the psychological apocalypse,"[37] the delusion that one can change other people, that the individual is anything beyond one's self. Pursuing "the wrong aspiration fantasy"[38] leads to what his disciple Wynne calls being "dragged down by write-offs."[39] Wynne and Hal are easy converts. Lars's real obstacles are the skeptics, such as his own wife who mocks his philosophy by naming her main course, the ultimate of her creations, "Apocalypse of Lobster."[40] He has to overcome her for, in her husband's view, Paige is a "centre of negativity, actively destructive of all that's around."[41] The uninvited guest Mike proves difficult too.

The playwright pegs Lars early in the play when he tells Hal that if you want peace and freedom and passion—who wouldn't?—not to mention "the eternal moment of present," you "simply abandon yourself to our most powerful instinct, the instinct of I Want," the only certain product of "the sensual world."[42] The prospect is, for many audiences, both absurd, and thereby comic, and yet chilling.

If his wife's objective is to control the dinner, the situation, even if it means her own death, Lars's is to change the group thinking, to make the dinner more than an occasion to celebrate his new book. So enamored by his philosophy of self, Lars can't sense the irony in Mike's questions: "Do you believe everything it says in your book?" And to Mike's "And you can control your own destiny and everything just by wanting it to happen?" Lars offers a seemingly humble, "I follow the primary life-force instinct."[43] Here, Lars meets the obstacles in Mike's "inquisition" by deflecting what would otherwise be his typical self-assertive answer: if he is controlled by a power greater than his own, it is one that is natural and therefore right. Paige sees through Lars's desperate need for self-justification when, toasting the author, she "boasts" that her husband's book has "outsold Delia Smith's *Cooking for the Brain Dead*."[44]

With his philosophy just barely concealing his need, a reverse mirror for that of his wife, the other six actors in the cast can then play off of Lars's obstacle; some defensively, others by capitulation, others still in opposition, ranging from Hal's tepid counterattack to the more aggressive campaigns of Paige and Mike — not to mention the Waiter.

Clarity of Expression: Hal

All the characters have their own vocabulary, with Paige and Lars setting the extremes, from dark, emotional wit to arrogant parody and comic rebuttals. Hal, the scientist, is clearly not comfortable with artists (Wynne purports to be one), philosophers, or TV personalities like Siân — the "rich cunts,"[45] in Mike's view, who round out the dinner party. Sometimes Hal can be socially awkward in his delivery. Unaware of Paige's sarcastic praise of the variety of Internet services available, he cannot detect the irony when she speaks of finding there "Siamese-twin prostitutes who'll dance naked in front of your friends." The actor might take Hal's "Is that what you've arranged for later?" as genuine, full of anticipation.[46]

He is the bumpkin at the dinner table, priding himself on what others probably take as infantile jokes. He asks Mike "What's the most interesting thing you've had in the back of your van?" and, without waiting for a reply, adds a dollop of (what he considers) wit with "Apart from your girlfriend, of course."[47] When he laughs at his own lame joke here, the other guests exchange knowing glances.

Hal is just as foolish when, straining to wax eloquent, he offers only a sort of linguistic overkill. He equates Lars's dogma to "dumb organisms vacuously multiplying, gormlessly devouring, pointlessly expiring. A hideous human death in each one of them." Fortunately he can't sustain the effort for long. Perhaps he tries to rival Lars as a wordsmith, but the attempt dies off with a clichéd simile at its end: "Like things you couldn't make up in a nightmare."[48] There is no poetry in his speech, even that born of sarcasm; no evidence that Hal can hold his own with the voluble talkers among the guests, especially the three women. And when he does try to insert a more sophisticated vocabulary into the

conversation, we get, instead, bad poetry that might have come out of
the Beat Generation.

Jealous that Paige has been enlisted by Mike as a fellow thief, Hal
struggles to carve out a place for himself: "I'd love a bit of stealth, bit
of ducking and driving, dodging and weaving, breaking and entering,
you know what I mean?"[49] Mike promptly turns him down, but not
discouraged, though now without words, Hal mimes a sniper firing "*an
imaginary machine gun at all the characters*," then singling out his wife
with "*a long volley*." As the intended target "*continues to devour her
lobster*," Hal, in a revealing stage direction, "*runs out of steam*."[50]

He asks Siân, who, he claims, is on television only because she's
sexy, why she "undermine[s him]" in front of his friends. This time,
she doesn't resort to her typical bitter wit or shock language, but, in
simple prose, nails his character: "I don't know who you are! I don't
even know what *job* you do. Who the *fuck* are you, Hal?" When he
attempts to answer ("I told you about my—"), she exits, and Hal, the
dullest of the five guests and so inadequate concerning language, is
further reduced to a single "Shit." Once again, Paige mercifully calls
for more drinks.[51]

The actor will want to examine all of Hal's lines, for his prose (from
the inarticulate to his bad poetry), his style of delivery, and his inability to
listen, to grasp what other says, especially the humor and sarcasm so
rife at the dinner table—these faults define him. The other characters are
in part revealed by their gestures, their movement, their body language.
But for Hal, it is more his words. He is something of the pantaloon of
the old comedy, out of the loop, what one actor calls "the deadener"
whose clumsy attempts at being convivial stops conversation in its
tracks. Possibly there is a parallel, after all, between two such otherwise
different characters as Lars and Hal: both are comically unaware how
absurd they are. The other actors will want to play off of Hal's speaking
style, filling out the gamut of such styles represented around the table.

Joke Structure/Comedic Timing: Siân

Siân's way of joking is most obvious in an interchange she has with
Wynne. Emboldened by Lars's argument that her art is not appreciated
because she is too "figurative," that she "doesn't just make crap out
of crap and call it art," Wynne turns with icy politeness to Siân, whom

she sees as a rival, and asks archly, "So, what do you like?" She may be expecting that Siân's tastes turn to kitsch, or even that she has no opinion or cannot understand the question. Instead, Siân replies, with a touch of false innocence, "I like the graffiti on the back of toilet doors." Then, amplifying the shock answer, she adds "I saw some today that said Fuck Shit Up," before turning the question back to Wynne with "Is that art?"[52] Paige's response—whether supportive or mocking being up to the actor—seals Siân's comic retort: "It's literature." Wynne now gangs up with Hal in dismissing her rival as a "newsbabe"; Siân, in turn, tricks them by seemingly playing into their hands with "I decorate the rolling news."[53] Missing the hostess's irony in her need to put down her rival, encouraged by what she thinks is a confirmation, Wynne cannot keep from the fray: "And gosh—it must cost you a fortune in suits." As if tiring with battling an unworthy opponent, Siân cuts her off with "I get an allowance,"[54] and then ignores Wynne. When Paige tries to embarrass Siân as she goes to one of the "two little girls' rooms" with "you probably want some mouthwash," Siân tops her with "I'd like a piss actually."[55] Siân's style is not to initiate a joke, but rather to refashion the bias of the character unwittingly setting her up. At other times, she enjoys throwing in a crude remark to what is otherwise witty upper-class dinner conversation.

And as she gains confidence, realizing her competitors are not as witty or as powerful as they think they are, she takes her particular humor to a deeper level, both in her delivery and in her contribution to the topics for the evening. Reacting to Paige's fashionable put-down of humans as being "once such persistent slime" when she explains how her primordial soup takes us back to our original selves, Siân adds to Lars's shallow "Bravo" the cryptic, possibly even poetic "Slime is the agony of water."[56] Are the four characters thrown by this unusual metaphor? Does Hal speak for the group's amazement at what has just come out of a newsbabe's mouth with his incredulous "What?" However you play it, Siân pushes her aphorism even further by name-dropping "Sartre," eliciting a second "What?" from Hal. As if signaling that the brainless sexpot has only been playing a role she's assumed to bait the other guests, at this moment a new character enters—Mike—who, like her, is not what the guests think he is, who is more profound that his blue-collar appearance would indicate—at least to them.

Siân's cryptic humor inoculates her from the barbs so endemic to the guests' table talk, even as it adds to their uncertainty about her identity. Actors can play off Siân's retorts, thereby sharpening their own character's comic style. Surely, the last thing you want in a show like this is for the characters to share a single way with jokes and put-downs. A good rehearsal game might involve asking each actor in character to make a joke about the same topic or situation.

Too Real, Not Real Enough: Mike

This category originally applied to an actor's navigating between being too natural and too mannered. However, "too real, not real enough" takes on a special meaning in Mike's case.

A stranger confronted with these upper-class poseurs, Mike has something of real life with him. Practical, very mundane matters bring him onstage: his van has broken down and he needs to use the phone to call a tow truck. Mike is blue collar; as Paige reminds him, "It's been years since any of us spoke to anyone working class."[57]

His speaking style and vocabulary are correspondingly simple, direct. It's ironic he takes the chair reserved for Bob, the no-show politician–actor. Mike calls them as he sees them. Not the thief he claims to be as he plays a lengthy joke on the other guests, he is "a nobody who does a shit-boring job":[58] Mike drives a van for a company in King's Cross (a relatively run-down district of London) "that mass-produces cakes."[59] Asked why he had to lie to the guests, he replies, "I didn't feel I had to. I just wanted to," and this explanation reveals at once his object:

> Supposing it was my aspirational fantasy to come here and join your party tonight? . . . I thought I could change my life by eating with your kind and shining people here? That if I was to sit with you at your table, I'd somehow leave a different man?[60]
>
> (Scene Three, The Main)

But his "aspirational fantasy" (reusing Lars's very term) turns out to be an illusion. He finds the guests "hollow and lost and alone [and] . . . for all their glittering ideas . . . twice as empty and miserable" as himself. In his blunt street talk, they have turned out "to be shit in [his] hands."[61]

Mike has been called "the most normal person at this table"; someone who, like the hostess in her way, can see through "the façade of the other characters to the hollow and lost confusion underneath."[62] Only Paige can answer his question of what the characters do with the "waste product [of] experience": "Pull the chain and forget it existed."[63] And it is telling that, of all the characters, she is the one he chose to join him in the criminal's trade. He also compliments Siân as "being on the side of truth" despite her TV work.[64] Mike sees high society for what it really is. The most devastating targets of his criticism come when he calls Lars "a rich cunt"[65] and tells Wynne that the married man she throws herself at is "Frozen Waste" and "fucking sterile."[66] Lars also becomes the main subject of his most extended joke, or rather a joke about the act of joking: "There was once a woman who married a block of ice, thinking that it was a man." When Lars asks for the punch line, Mike shoots back: "There isn't one. It's just a fucking joke."[67]

To play with our own terms, Mike is "real enough," yet not too real. Some have seen a touch of the playwright in him, Buffini's representative attacking the vapid British upper class. Once he sheds his role as thief, he becomes a modern-day Everyman chronicling the slow, mostly self-inflicted death of what now passes for the aristocracy. Predictably, he has a special status for the guests. As he takes the empty seat at the table, "Jesus' chair" as Paige has called it,[68] she tells him, "We're all dying to know if you think we're redeemable."[69] Mike pulls the Truth card in the game his hostess has devised for when conversation falters.

Besides coming to a decision about the degree to which Mike is "real" or "unreal" (symbolic, allegorical perhaps?), the actor will want to have his style of delivery parallel this real/unreal duality in the character. Too real, as if he were talking in the street, as if he were not acting, and that symbolic status might be dulled. Conversely, the actor does not want Mike to be too mannered, marked by an oratorical style that would detract from the sense of ordinary life that he brings with him to challenge the surreal atmosphere of Paige's dinner party. Consider the categories we've examined so far in bringing Mike to life. Give him a history. What has his life been like? His family? His father especially? We have cited his self-announced objective in barging into the dinner party—what obstacle, then, did he imagine he might overcome by doing so, and by posing as a thief? How is Mike's humor like that of Paige, his prospective criminal compatriot as he sees her? Or Siân's?

If the formulaic dinner-party comedy calls for an unexpected arrival, the uninvited guest, how can the actor make Mike something more than the generic stereotype?

Your Self and Your Comic Character: Wynne

Wynne, who styles herself as an "eroticist" eager to share her "feelings [physical as well as emotional?] with the world,"[70] also compares herself to the artist Gustav Klimt who, like her, is also a "provocative eroticist."[71] She has generated a somewhat mixed reaction from actors and reviewers. Catherine Usher sees her as "the adorable dippy hippy."[72] The Warwick play guide calls her "sweet, honest, and a little bit mad."[73] Jessica Fostekew, however, lumps Wynne with the others, as being "as big a cretinous snob as her companions."[74]

She charges onto the stage, having been buffeted by the fog and, worse yet, rejected by her lover Bob. Her crime, in his eyes, was painting and then exhibiting a portrait of his genitals with the unimaginative title, "Bob Patterson's Cock," then defending the work as "impressionistic" and possessed of a "dreamlike quality."[75] She still loves Lars because his writings allow her to "free oneself from liability, from blame."[76]

So, here we have an artist, or rather a wannabe artist, who seeks escape from a dull life through her craft. She is pretentious without meaning to be so. Eager to share her feelings, she pivots from her art to Lars and his pseudo-philosophy and, later, to Mike.

She uses memories of the past to shape her present. After recalling the death of her mother years ago, Wynne reminds everybody that, thanks to Lars's book, she is now in "a good place." To get there, she takes comfort in Lars's dubious paradox: "Nothing enhances life more than death."[77]

Once she gets into her artist bent, nothing can stop her. In her longest speech in the play, she first rejects painting death as "Byronic in a dark suit," substituting instead death wearing "Hugo Boss." Then she erases this portrait by borrowing Lars's vacuous abstractions that "death is nothing" and that "nothing is everything." But she can't help reverting to character, concluding that death has to be "the biggest orgasm one ever has / That's all. The end." When Lars compliments her with "You're right," she modestly claims it was a "bit waffly"—perhaps the truest words she utters in the play.[78]

If you were playing Wynne, you might want to ask yourself what past experiences, feelings, needs, and desires you could call up to get into the role. However, such memories should not keep you from focusing on the character's object: for Wynne, "undiscovered as yet,"[79] it might be proving herself an artist, or getting into the circle of her intellectual superiors by endorsing Lars's book. Or maybe she wants to contribute something to the gathering darkness of the evening as it looms toward the final course: "Desserts. Just desserts."[80] How might these memories help in fashioning your Wynne—real, but not too real—and, again, allow you to keep in mind her *objective* in the play?

Body Awareness: The Waiter

The character with almost no lines until the end, the Waiter is as central to the play as the talkative dinner guests. Any actor given his part would surely want to make him as interesting and as vital as possible. For most of *Dinner*, he must do this with his movements, his gestures, his facial expressions. It is more than difficult to be onstage without lines. To speak in his silence—this is what the Waiter has to do. That silence can raise the audience's curiosity. Will he do more than just serve the chatty guests, or answer Paige's numerous calls for drinks? Note that at the start of the play, he stands "*on the edge of the light*," and as Paige approaches, she kisses him, then puts a "*thickly stuffed envelope into his pocket.*"[81] She is gruff with him, as we might expect a nervous hostess to be, yet that kiss remains intriguing, unsettling. She calls him repeatedly for drinks, or to serve the next course, and he always arrives on cue. Some actors might want to have him anticipate her orders and be standing behind her as she calls, as if he were just offstage. His entrances and exits seem like numerous beats in the dialogue, marking shifts in the exchanges among the guests. When Hal warns Lars they "can't go there" (i.e., discuss Hal's dead wife Mags), the Waiter "*enters with crockery for soup* [and] *sets it at the table.*"[82] When Wynne chides Hal for "looking for mutancy and hideous disease,"[83] again the Waiter enters, this time with the Parmesan cheese Lars has ordered. And it is the Waiter who underscores Paige's rationalization of her life— "I do nothing. I never have"[84]—by entering with drinks and serving them. When Paige announces they are "ready for the main," the most excruciating stage of her four-part meal, the Waiter gets to "*nod* [. . .]" before exiting.[85]

In the Warwick production, when the company held separate rehearsals for the backstage crew, the Waiter always attended—indeed, he was seen as "an integral part" of the team. Their aim was to help him make his "service as efficient as it needs to be."[86] When he serves the guests, there are lots of options for the actor. Can he be positioned so that he observes them without being seen? Is he like a silent Greek chorus between the stage and the audience? Might he share with us his feelings by gestures, facial expressions, his various moves around the table? To be direct, what does he think about what is going on? What is his history with Paige? When did they arrange for him to assist in her suicide? Asking such questions, raising such possibilities for a mostly silent character, gives a special significance to what we have called "body awareness."

Just before the final scene, Paige calls out, "Where's the waiter?" and—surprisingly—he answers, "I'm here." She "*takes the Waiter's hand*" and, on her ominous "Let's do as we arranged," which the guests take as a command to bring on the final course, "Just desserts," he bows and exits.[87]

In the final scene, as "arranged," he helps Paige fulfill her fantasy about death: that it is the ultimate test of one's control in life, the final obstacle to overcome. As he stabs Paige, in a series of actions for which his earlier entrances, exits, and serving now seems like a pale prelude, the Waiter puts his hand on her forehead with the "*compassion* [Hal had used this word when arguing with Lars in Scene One] *and authority of a priest*." He stands, pulls the handkerchief from his pocket, and wipes the blade. When Mike lunges at him, the Waiter "*raises a hand*," stopping him "*in his tracks*." He removes the envelope of money from his pocket. To Lars's "Who are you?" the Waiter, as he "*takes two banknotes from the top of the pile*," replies in his most extensive speech in the play: "My service is free / I take only the wage of a waiter." He bows. He leaves. Mike chases after him.[88]

A Coda on the Ending

With minimal, indeed sparse dialogue, whatever the actor has brought to his character—a history, playing obstacles, clarity of diction, joke timing, body awareness, affective or emotional memory—will now bear fruit in the final moments of this black comedy. We are left with the quintet of guests, each with a telling line that becomes the actor's signature to the character he or she has fashioned.

Lars, in response to Wynne's "What can I do?" answers simply, "Nothing." Hal, lacking the necessary linguistic dexterity, breaks into a sort of child-like poetry: "The fog seems to be / I mean / In the house." Siân is reduced to two words—"Freezing" and later, "Cold"—"like a TV weatherwoman." Mike has his characteristic basic speech, but his line ends with a poetic cadence: "I couldn't find him / He just vanished / It was like / No sound, nothing." When "*the lights flicker*," Wynne calls out to some unseen god—or is it just the light board operator? "Give us the light back / Give us light." Then we hear a collective "*Breathing*" (the sources of speech? Like warm-up exercise, as one actor observed) and the otherwise silent stage offers "*A palpable sense of fear*." Lars, proponent of the "I Want" school of self-improvement, the power of positive thinking, offers the verdict: "Nothing."[89]

* * *

By working through these suggested basic "rules" alongside a script, actors can form their internal and external characters in sync with the plot arc and other characters. This is the "craft" of acting comedy referenced in this book's subtitle. In Chapter 1, laughter was not just a theme in Reza's play *"Art"* but the source of conflict between friends— and its resolution. Laughter, both among the characters and from the audience, complemented the chapter's focus on the questions of how we laugh and why—on what laughter can mean. In the current chapter, we used the play *Dinner* to explore how the "craft" of acting—how actors, enacting the playwright's characters—can make an audience laugh. In effect, we've moved from the "art" of comedy in Chapter 1 (appropriately, with a play of the same name) to its practical application here in Chapter 3, with the "craft" of comedy when those practical rules are applied to *Dinner*.

In the next chapter, titled "Elements of the Comic Character," the characters themselves are the subject. The word "elements" refers to what might also be called "the psychology of the comic character." Or, to use an outmoded word, what makes the comic character *tick*? We speak of a comic character's world as one in which he confronts incongruities and opposites, underreacts and overreacts to situations, experiences status shifts or collapses of dignity, is handicapped by childishness or self-ignorance, or is given to rapidly changing emotions and hypervulnerability. Knowing what is at the heart of the comic character, what drives him, and why he takes seriously a world that we may find silly, insane, or absurd, an assault on what is normal and rational, is the key for the actor charged with the role. Chapter 4 unlocks how this key can be utilized, referring to three comedies: Christopher Durang's *Beyond Therapy* and two short plays by John Pielmeier, *Cheek to Cheek* and *Goober's Descent*.

Notes

1   John A. Ferraro, quoted in "Hamlet's Buddies," *Alameda Times-Star*, July 15, 1998.

2   Lawrence Parke, *Since Stanislavski and Vakhtangov: The Method as a System for Today's Actor* (Hollywood: Acting World Books, 1985), 250–1; see also François-Joseph Talma, "Grandeur Without Pomp," in *Actors on Acting: The Theories, Techniques, and Practices of the Great Actors of all Times as Told in Their Own Words*, ed. Toby Cole and Helen Krich Chinoy (New York: Crown Publishers, 1949).

3   François-Joseph Talma, "Reflections on Acting," in *Papers on Acting*, ed. Brander Matthews (New York: Hill and Wang, 1958), 183.

4   Paul Ryan, *The Art of Comedy: Getting Serious about Being Funny* (New York: Back Stage Books, 2007), 8–11.

5   Constantin Stanislavski, *An Actor Prepares* (New York: Routledge/Theatre Arts Books, 1936), 150–1.

6   Gavin Levy, *275 Acting Games: Connected: A Comprehensive Workbook of Theatre Games for Developing Acting Skills* (Colorado Springs: Meriwether Publishing, 2010), 245–6.

7   Henning Nelms, *Play Production: A Handbook for the Backstage Worker, a Guidebook for the Student of Drama* (New York: Barnes and Noble, 1950), 159.

8   Ibid., 165–6.

9   Parke, *Since Stanislavski and Vakhtangov*, 248.

10 Ibid., 250.

11 Stuart Vaughan, *Directing Plays: A Working Professional's Method* (New York: Longman, 1993), 254.

12 Ibid., 222.

13 Henry Irving, in *Theatre, Culture and Society: Essays, Addresses and Lectures*, ed. Jeffrey Richards (Keele, UK: Keele University Press, 1994), 72.

14 Maria Aitken, *Style: Acting in High Comedy* (New York: Applause Books, 1996), 111.
15 Doug Moston, *Coming to Terms with Acting: An Instructive Glossary* (New York: Drama Book Publishers, 1993), 31.
16 Henri Szeps, *All in Good Timing: A Personal Account of What an Actor Does* (Sydney: Currency Press, 1996), 32–3.
17 Ibid.
18 Ibid.
19 See Brian Clover, "*Dinner* Now Being Served at the Wyndham," review of *Dinner*, *CurtainUp*, December 10, 2003, http://www.curtainup.com/dinner.html (accessed July 1, 2016).
20 Moira Buffini, *Dinner* (London: Faber and Faber, 2002), 21.
21 Ibid., 22.
22 Ibid., 13.
23 Ibid., 10.
24 Lyn Gardner, review of *Dinner*, *The Guardian*, Theatre section, December 11, 2003.
25 Buffini, *Dinner*, 4.
26 Ibid., 81.
27 Ibid., 3.
28 Ibid., 6.
29 Ibid., 45.
30 Ibid., 11.
31 Ibid., 74.
32 Ibid., 57.
33 Ibid.
34 Ibid., 59.
35 Ibid., 81.
36 Ibid., 105.
37 Ibid., 22.
38 Ibid., 53.
39 Ibid., 12.
40 Ibid., 56.
41 Ibid., 96.
42 Ibid., 25.
43 Ibid., 77.
44 Ibid., 18.
45 Ibid., 40.
46 Ibid., 19.
47 Ibid., 43.
48 Ibid., 20–1.
49 Ibid., 64.
50 Ibid.
51 Ibid., 83–4.

52 Ibid., 15.

53 Ibid., 16.

54 Ibid.

55 Ibid., 19.

56 Ibid., 34.

57 Ibid., 51.

58 Ibid., 76.

59 Ibid., 75.

60 Ibid., 78.

61 Ibid.

62 Tech Crew: Warwick Arts Centre, "Moira Buffini's *Dinner*" (submission pack, Warwick Arts Centre Studio, autumn term, 2007), www.wuds. co.uk/submissions/Dinner.doc (accessed July 1, 2016).

63 Buffini, *Dinner*, 79.

64 Ibid., 45.

65 Ibid., 96.

66 Ibid., 99.

67 Ibid., 96.

68 Ibid., 27.

69 Ibid., 42.

70 Ibid., 10.

71 Ibid., 49.

72 Catherine Usher, review of *Dinner*, *The Stage*, February 15, 2008, in Lainey Shaw's online portfolio, Reviews section, http://www.laineyshaw. co.uk/reviews/Dinner Reviews March 2008.doc (accessed July 1, 2016).

73 Tech Crew: Warwick Arts Centre, "Moira Buffini's *Dinner*."

74 Jessica Fostekew, "Intimate Party with Comical Thrills," review of *Dinner*, February 13, 2008, http://www.remotegoat.com/uk/review/1181/intimate-party-with-comical-thrills/#reviews (accessed July 1, 2016).

75 Buffini, *Dinner*, 10.

76 Ibid., 12.

77 Ibid., 87.

78 Ibid., 88.

79 Ibid., 15.

80 Ibid., 93.

81 Ibid., 3.

82 Ibid., 20.

83 Ibid., 31.

84 Ibid., 62.

85 Ibid., 47.

86 Tech Crew: Warwick Arts Centre, "Moira Buffini's *Dinner*."

87 Buffini, *Dinner*, 93.

88 Ibid., 105–6.

89 Ibid., 106–7.

4
ELEMENTS OF THE COMIC CHARACTER

Even though it is essential that comic characters be grounded in reality, to increase the laughs the comedic actor needs to be aware of a number of devices and age-old tricks. In this chapter, we will guide you through over- and underreacting, playing incongruity and opposites, applied childishness, rapidly changing emotions, hypervulnerability, status shifts, collapses of dignity, and self-ignorance. The comedic actor should work to incorporate these elements, when possible, into his characterization. They are not mutually exclusive, and, at any point, two or more may be operating simultaneously. Often, the actor will have a choice of which element, or elements, to emphasize. The audience, through their laughter, ratify the choice, completing the circle from stage to house.

"Go for that kind of comedy that is based in character and real feelings,"[1] advised Christopher Durang in his Author's Notes to *Beyond Therapy*, wherein he also cited fellow playwright Joe Orton's production note for *Ruffian on the Stair*: "Every one of the characters must be real. None of them is ever consciously funny … The most ludicrous lines … must be played quite sincerely. Unless it's real it won't be funny."[2] Durang's opening scene in *Beyond Therapy* illustrates this perfectly. Bruce is seated at a restaurant table, looking at his watch. Prudence enters, and, "*after hesitating a moment*," crosses to him:

Prudence Hello.
Bruce Hello.
Prudence (*perhaps referring to a newspaper in her hand—The New York Review of Books?*) Are you the white male, 30 to

35, 6'2", blue eyes, who's into rock music, movies, jogging, and quiet evenings at home?

Bruce Yes, I am. (*Stands.*)

Prudence Hi, I'm Prudence.

Bruce I'm Bruce.

Prudence Nice to meet you.

Bruce Won't you sit down?

Prudence Thank you. (*Sits.*) As I said in my letter, I've never answered one of these ads before.

Bruce Me neither. I mean, I haven't put one in before.

Prudence But this time I figured, why not?

Bruce Right. Me too. (*Pause.*) I hope I'm not too macho for you.

Prudence No. So far you seem wonderful.

Bruce You have lovely breasts. That's the first thing I notice in a woman.

Prudence Thank you.

Bruce You have beautiful contact lenses.

Prudence Thank you. I like the timbre of your voice. Soft but firm.

Bruce Thanks. I like *your* voice.

Prudence Thank you. I love the smell of the Brut you're wearing.

Bruce Thank you. My male lover Bob gave it to me.

Prudence What?

Bruce You remind me of him in a certain light.

Prudence What?

Bruce I swing both ways actually. Do you?

Prudence (*rattled, serious*) I don't know. I always insist on the lights being out.

Pause.

Bruce I'm afraid I've upset you now.

Prudence No, it's nothing really. It's just that I hate gay people.

Bruce I'm not gay. I'm bisexual. There's a difference.

Prudence I don't really know any bisexuals.

[. . .]

Bruce *cries.*

Prudence (*continued*) *Please*, don't cry, please.

Bruce (*stops crying after a bit*) I feel better after that. You have a lovely mouth.

Prudence Thank you.

Bruce I can tell you're sensitive. I want you to have my children.
Prudence Thank you.
Bruce Do you feel ready to make a commitment?
Prudence I feel I need to get to know you better.
Bruce I feel we agree on all the issues. I feel that you like rock
    music, movies, jogging, and quiet evenings at home. I think you
    hate shallowness. I bet you never read "People" magazine.
Prudence I do read it. I write for it.
Bruce I write for it too. Freelance actually. I send in letters. They
    printed one of them.
Prudence Oh, what was it about?
Bruce I wanted to see Gary Gilmore executed on television.
Prudence Oh, yes, I remember that one.
Bruce Did you identify with Jill Clayburgh in "An Unmarried
    Woman"?
Prudence Uh, yes, I did.
Bruce Me too! We agree on everything. I want to cry again.
Prudence I don't like men to cry. I want them to be strong.[3]

(Act One, Scene One)

Overreacting and Underreacting

Here, as in most comedies, a character's overreaction is an essential
element in signaling the triviality of events to the audience, giving them
permission to laugh. But such overreaction must always be grounded
in the character's needs. Otherwise, it becomes mere clowning or
caricature. Acting teacher Doug Moston maintained that only if they
perceive the incongruity between the small event and the big overreaction
will the audience respond to the humor grounded in this disparity.[4]
Again, *Beyond Therapy* illustrates this well. There must be incredibly high
stakes for the comedy to work, and the more the actors can maintain
their emotionally amplified attempts to get what they need—namely, "to
salvage the evening"—the funnier they will seem to us.

Bruce, a particularly volatile and explosive character, is prone to
overreaction throughout the play. However absurd or incomprehensible
his dialogue, he believes passionately in everything he says. He is
neurotic and endures wild mood swings. One moment his feelings

are hurt and he's crying hysterically, and the next he's passionately imploring Prudence to marry him and start a family. Prudence is an equally complex character: she goes on a blind date, even though she's fearful it will be just another wasted night. Yet she desperately wants to find someone to share her life with. Intrigued by Bruce's ad, she is excited, optimistic even, but still fraught with doubts. Embarrassed by having to resort to a personal ad, Bruce is just as eager and desperate as Prudence. The point again is that, the more amplified the needs, and the higher the characters' expectations, the more there will be to lose and this loss will allow for more conflict and thus more laughter from the house. It is the breakdown of the characters' expectations and then the resulting discomfort they experience that creates the tension and therefore the humor of the scene. The worse the date gets, the funnier it is to watch.

Like overreacting, underreacting is based on the incongruity between the given circumstances and the actor's reaction to them. In underreacting, the character *should* behave more intensely yet does not, either because such underreacting is part of his makeup or because the character purposely underreacts trying to conceal his true feelings. Attempting to be casual, both Bruce and Prudence hide their anxiety under a glib delivery. Overreacting might expose their denials; underreacting, especially "exaggerated" underreacting, might prove too thin a cover for their true feelings. However, within seconds, this façade will crumble for Bruce when he tells Prudence she has "lovely breasts."

Whatever choice the actors make, overreacting or underreacting, they win by keeping us on our toes, never sure which way they will turn. The combination of the two extremes gets a laugh from the audience—again, as long as the choice fits with our initial take on the two. When Bruce reveals that he is a bisexual, he goes too far by asking what Prudence takes as an invasion of her privacy: "I swing both ways. Do you?" Durang notes that her ambiguous response, "I don't know," is "*Rattled, serious.*" For this woman is afraid of commitments, and Bruce threatens to expose her private life, his question going beyond the bounds of what is deemed polite conversation. But once Bruce mentions his male lover Bob, he becomes bolder and this leads to asking Prudence about her sex life. No wonder she is "*serious*" and "*rattled*." The question surprises and confuses her. The actor must make a choice at this point: she can either underreact as a way of steering the conversation toward a less provocative topic, or she can *pretend* to underreact in order not to appear unworldly or narrow-minded. So far in the conversation she has been more guarded, and by playing it this way, she goes from overreacting to underreacting without a beat.

In fact, underreaction might be a dominant trait in Prudence—at least in the early stages of the play. And because Bruce overreacts, they "feed" each other. His need may be to assert himself, especially over what he perceives as a more passive woman. Confronted with such an assertive male, she recedes even more into herself.

When Bruce jumps from discussing the ad to a boldly implied question "I'm not too macho for you?" he should blurt this out, because the semi-question comes from deep inside himself. He fears he is coming on too strong and only compounds the fear by, well, coming on too strong. He overreacts. But notice that she underreacts with the banal "No. So far you seem wonderful." It's his "macho" against her "wonderful."

Playing Incongruity and Opposites

Incongruity involves a reversal of expectation. The audience anticipates one thing but gets something else; the humor lies in the incompatibility between the two. It follows then that the actor should seek to increase those moments by behaving in the opposite way to what the audience anticipates.

Human beings are complex entities, laughing when they should cry, crying when they should laugh. Since people can be wholly unpredictable, why should comedic characters be any different? The actor has to assume a collaborative role with the playwright in choosing opposite traits for the character, because their presence guarantees both internal and external conflicts—conflicts that intrigue the audience and thereby drive the show. The playwright and teacher Lajos Egri suggested that the "contradictions within a man and the contradictions around him create a decision and a conflict [and that these] in turn force him into a new decision and a new conflict."[5]

When an actor offers a stock response, a clichéd action, the audience often experience a disconnect and lose focus. They realize they're only in a theatre, only watching a performance. But, when the actor plays the opposite choice from what they expect, that same audience is surprised, and therefore brought back, reconnected, to the life onstage. Michael Shurtleff devoted an entire chapter in his book *Audition* to what is known as "playing the opposite,"[6] and suggested that if the actor has an impulse to do something onstage, he or she should always consider doing the opposite. Why? Because, if an actor has an inclination to commit a specific action, the audience is oftentimes slightly ahead of him, since, in simultaneously processing the circumstances of the character and the events of the play, they are developing expectations about the emotions, behaviors, or courses of action that will follow. But if the actor chooses the opposite action from what they have deduced—if he whispers when the audience expects him to scream, if she sits when the audience expects her to stand—then the audience will be surprised, and delighted at *not* getting what they expect. This is what happens in *Beyond Therapy*'s opening scene, when the macho Bruce's crying so disturbs Prudence. Her ideal man doesn't cry. One of the many options for the actor is to make Bruce's cry an intense prolonged sob, so much so that it takes two "please"s from Prudence—the first italicized in the script—to stop him, and even then not right away, as the stage direction is that Bruce "*Stops crying* [only] *after a bit*." It's the incongruity of a grown man's crying so loudly and with such abandon that never fails to generate laughter from the audience *when* the actor balances that fine line between too much and not enough emotional truth. If he plays it too naturalistically, he might engage the audience's empathy, which would prevent them from laughing; not naturalistically enough, and the performance might be too superficial to generate the tension necessary for the comedy.

The moment the crying stops, Bruce pulls himself together with the justification that he "feel[s] better after doing so." Having watched him let out his feelings, the audience now expects Bruce, calmed down and chastened by Prudence, to return to the seemingly innocuous banter of the opening. But Durang gives him a fairly suggestive line: "You have a lovely mouth." That same "lovely" just might recall the clearly suggestive, disruptive line earlier: "You have lovely breasts." The actor should go from "feel better" to "lovely mouth" without a beat, the first delivered meekly, the second suggestively, erotically, changing from the sensitive man who disturbs Prudence with his crying to the "macho" fellow sitting opposite her, fixated on her breasts and mouth. While Durang described Bruce's bisexuality as "essential to [his] being funny,"[7] we might also take that word "bisexuality" as embracing the dual, contradictory, opposite dimensions of his character. He isn't just one thing but complex, as incongruous as humans tend to be.

The audience should always be kept in a state of tension between not knowing and wanting to know what will happen next. They should be kept guessing, suspecting that they are speculating without all the facts, because predictability is the death of comedy. In *Acting Skills for Life*, Ron Cameron pointed out that "unexpected events may happen at one of the following stages of action: (1) the setup, (2) the expectation of the action, (3) unfulfillment of an anticipated action."[8] Every joke contains a surprise, in that the audience is led to believe the joke will go one way, and then—"bang!"—it goes another, unexpected way.

Henri Szeps retold the story of Chaplin being asked by a student how best to film the sequence of a man slipping on a banana peel: "Chaplin said that he would first show the banana peel. Then he would cut to the man walking towards it. But before the man got to the banana peel he would suddenly disappear down a manhole."[9] For Szeps, the actor should "provide adequate decoys to continually surprise the audience— in other words, at each moment we point the audience's attention in the direction the play seems to be going, rather than where it is going."[10] Surprising the audience is what makes comedy work.

When Bruce tells Prudence he finds her "sensitive," we assume that, eager to win her over on this first date, he will then add another compliment or two. This is what we would expect. Instead, we get a surprise, as if Bruce has leapfrogged over the first date and is now in a long-term relationship with Prudence: "I want you to have my children." And Prudence's reply, that simple "Thank you," is no less a surprise, the same two words that seconds ago greeted his "You have a lovely mouth." What happens to the audience's reactions if the actress delivers both "thank you"s exactly the same, with the same signifying gesture? The play is only minutes old. We've witnessed one surprise already, at least for Prudence: Bruce's bisexuality. But now this? How, the audience may be asking, did we get from there to here so quickly? Surely, the situation is not realistic: it usually takes at least a string of dates before we ask someone to make a baby with us. And yet on stage this will seem real, be convincing, if the actors play characters who believe in what they say. Bruce is tired of the childless life with Bob, and Prudence, worried that her biological clock is ticking down (she will confess this later in the play), has answered his ad not just to date but also to find someone to father her children. The situation, the surprise, is as implausible and yet as human as can be!

As in the real world, there must continually be a new element of surprise in a character's encounters with his world. When the actor loses that sense of his character's surprise, then the illusion that things are happening for the first time is broken, and what the audience sees is an actor merely going through the motions. The audience will cease to believe — or, more accurately, they will cease to *disbelieve* — in both actor and character. This happens frequently during long runs of shows or productions that have been remounted.

Though given just one word of dialogue ("What?"), the actor playing Prudence must craft that word to show surprise when Bruce mentions his "male lover Bob" and then again when he tells her she reminds him of Bob "in a certain light." She will shortly announce that she "hate[s] gay people" and little wonder she is surprised by Bruce's confession: she was hoping he was straight. Durang speaks of Bruce's "innocence and genuine 50–50 sexuality";[11] if we take his "You remind me of him in a certain light" as a compliment with conviction, then Prudence's second "what" is no less a surprise, though of a different order. One word repeated, delivered two different ways, and thereby leading to two very distinct surprises for the characters and, no less, the audience.

Comedic characters usually rebound just a bit too quickly from defeat and degradation, from sadness and despair. Like children, their world can be ending dramatically one moment, and they can be perfectly happy and fine the next. As Shurtleff observed, "The unexpectedness of the use of opposites, not the telegraphing of them, is the lifeblood of the adept comedy player."[12] Maria Aitken, in *Style: Acting in High Comedy*, advised comic actors "to identify each change of feeling and to occupy each moment of that feeling to the hilt ... moving cleanly from one emotion to the next."[13] Comic characters surprise us by such rapid and constant changes in their moods. They're up, they're down, they are all over the emotional map. The audience laughs because of the incongruity between the ways a "normal" person is expected to act or react and the way the comedic character does.

Applied Childishness

One trait that comedians and comedic actors from Harpo Marx to Robin Williams share is the quality of being childlike. Szeps has asserted that all drama, and particularly comedy, is aimed at the "child" in us: "However sophisticated the thoughts of the play, however beautiful the poetry, however valid the moral arguments, it is only by touching the child in the members of the audience that they will be truly affected."[14]

Infants and children exist in a constant state of need, and they're not shy about letting you know. They want what they want *when* they want it. The intensity of their desires is often disproportionate to the situation, and so their reactions seem funny. Many of the most successful comedic actors have approached their roles with the intense desires of a child. Lucille Ball, as the character Lucy Ricardo, committed herself absolutely to the physical and emotional suffering of her character; the audience found it funny because she so exaggerated her pain that it was infantile in proportion. Think of her on the factory assembly line, trying to keep up with candy whizzing by on the conveyor belt. Or her exaggerated crying when she didn't get what she wanted from her husband Ricky Ricardo. When things, anything, didn't go her way, she bawled like a baby, pushing the intensity of her emotions into the realm of the ridiculous while her behavior was still firmly rooted in human reality.

Jason Alexander on television's *Seinfeld* is another good example of an actor using infantile behavior for comedic effect. Even though he was in his thirties, in his character George Costanza he was able to continuously tap into the selfish, intense, needy, and shallow child within himself for hilarious results. The lesson to be learned from artists like Lucille Ball and Jason Alexander is that when your character does not get what he or she wants, all hell should break loose. Want like a child; the bigger, the better.

Rapidly Changing Emotions

Rapid and incongruous shifts in emotion are a convention in comedy; they surprise and amuse the audience. It's a relief to laugh at someone so volatile, so consumed by conflicting emotions. In comedy, as in drama generally, however, the fact that a character is laughing one moment and crying the next must still be justified by the character's overall (psychological, emotional, physiological) makeup. The oddity of an adult acting like a child is funny because "normally" only children are allowed such open, uncensored, rapidly changing expression of their feelings. Adults are expected to restrain themselves; when they act like children, they create a surprising incongruity that leads to laughter.

Look at this exchange between two characters simply designated as "HE" and "SHE" in John Pielmeier's *Cheek to Cheek*.[15] They meet on the dance floor at a wedding. After an exchange of pleasantries, complications set in: SHE starts to cry, the reason at first unspecified; HE's marrying Cecilia, but is still in love with SHE; SHE's married to Michael but the marriage is a sham, for SHE still loves HE and, besides, Michael is moving in with Roger; Cecilia has had an affair with Michael; SHE's pregnant, but with Roger's baby.

SHE Am I succeeding [in making him jealous]?

HE Not in the least. Chances are, *if* you're pregnant *at all*, the kid's mine.

SHE Guess again.

HE You're certain of that?

SHE Absolutely positive.

HE Good. I wouldn't have wanted it anyway. (*She kicks him.*) Ow!

SHE Sorry.

HE Tramp.

SHE It happened the week you were away with Cathy.

HE Who told you about Cathy?

SHE *Everybody* knew.

HE Jealous?

SHE Not in the least. (*A beat.*) Besides, with your little problem, there's no way you could be *anybody's* father.

HE That only happened a few times.

SHE Did your little difficulty "come up," if you'll pardon the expression, with Cathy?

HE We both had a wonderful time, if you take my meaning.

SHE Funny. That's not what *she* says.

HE The only woman with whom I've had *any* problem is *you.*

SHE Roger had no trouble at all when *he* was with me, and he's a twit.

HE He must have been staring at your mustache. (*A beat.*)

SHE Ape.

HE Medusa.

SHE Ogre.

HE Witch.

SHE Idiot.

HE Delilah.

SHE Liar!

HE Liar!

BOTH Hate! I hate you! Hate! Ugly! You're an ape! You're disgusting! Stupid! Baby! You're a big baby! I hate your guts! (*Suddenly they notice people are watching, and, embarrassed, they apologize simultaneously.*)[16]

(Act One)

HE goes through a series of emotional jumps that are lightning fast, extreme, and, most obviously, do not grow out of any extended dialogue with SHE. HE moves from confidence to doubt, to name-calling, puzzlement, then pleasure, recoiling, denying, and finally degenerating again to name-calling.

The series of such emotional jumps that SHE goes through are no less varied. In the course of the short play, at first SHE seems happy for the newlyweds, then SHE moves into sadness, despair, anger, rage, and embarrassment, until finally, at the end of the play, SHE joins HE in the most sudden and comical switch of all, a state of loving adoration:

HE Too much to drink.

SHE Just a silly game.

They dance together in silence, poised and formal again.

HE How's your mother?

SHE Very well, thank you. And yours?

HE Very happy. (*A beat. They both begin to cry.*) God, I love you.

SHE I love *you*.

HE When can we see each other again?

SHE Right after the honeymoon?

HE Why wait?

SHE I can't.
HE Book a passage on the boat with us.
SHE I already have.
HE Tomorrow night. Ten o'clock. Poop deck.
SHE It's a date.
HE Darling.
SHE Sweetheart (*The music ends.*) Thank you for the dance.[17]

(Act One)

This scene is a real challenge for any comic actor, since all these changes occur in just three pages. Meet the challenge and the audience will laugh even though the situation is highly improbable.

Hypervulnerability

Most of us construct identities for ourselves that omit the negative, that suppress or keep hidden a darker, wilder, more libidinal side. As humans living in a society, we cannot accommodate this darker side, but as actors we cannot do without it. As directors, we see it all the time: actors who only want to be nice, cute, or charming onstage, so that everyone in the audience will love them. Meanwhile, they keep that hateful, infantile monster carefully concealed, even when the text calls for such a characterization.

But comedic actors must be willing and able to display in front of an audience the side of themselves that most of us prefer to keep hidden. Sometimes inexperienced actors try to hide their vulnerability in physical ways. The temptation simply to turn upstage is always great, as is closing the eyes, or putting the face down or in the hands. Mumbling lines or speaking at low volume are also signs of obscuring the real emotional life of both the actor and the character. Those actors who only want to be charming onstage deny the true craft of characterization when the text calls out for it. Comedy actors, especially, must possess an openness, a willingness to be vulnerable, and, most of all, trust in the audience to separate actor from character.

There is a paradox in acting: to create a complex, multidimensional character, the actor must make choices about the character's defense mechanisms—the ways the character protects himself or herself from the external world through denial, sublimation, or identification. At the same time, the actor has to lower his own defenses and open up emotionally. In Pielmeier's short play, the defensive structures for HE and SHE are paper-thin, yet they expose their emotions rapidly, bluntly, and without shame. In real life, the two actors would likely express such emotions in a more sophisticated, guarded, "adult" (and "less childish") way. Only the surreal, absurdly comic exchange in the play distinguishes the emotions of HE and SHE from what we—actor and audience—know offstage; the dialogue onstage requires that the actors, albeit under the protective guise of the characters, expose what they know is already in themselves. It is a very difficult thing, then, to bare oneself night after night in front of large groups of people. It takes practice and technique; the actor has to learn and "unlearn" his own characteristic defenses and strategies. In other words, the actor has to know and then avoid all the different ways that he "hides" from the audience. Thus, for our purposes, *Cheek to Cheek* can function both as a short play and as an actor's exercise in displaying this susceptibility.

On his deathbed, the eighteenth-century poet Alexander Pope is reported to have uttered "I have been a fool," while the nineteenth-century playwright Strindberg divulged "I have looked into myself and found Hell." Vulnerability—at the last!

Status Shift, Collapse of Dignity, and Self-Ignorance

In John Pielmeier's *Goober's Descent*,[18] the woman, a successful corporate executive, is working through a year-by-year list of the men who insulted or degraded her in the workplace on her way up. She is now bent on humiliating them in return. Goober's humiliation at the hands of his former secretary is the central subject of the play. By the end, he has been reduced from a smug and unctuous "macho man" to a degraded, half-naked submissive groveling at Stella's feet. After she has thoroughly belittled Goober and he has exited, she crosses him off the list, saying, "That takes care of '75."[19]

The audience thus gets to witness the deflation of an incredibly pompous male chauvinist at the hands of a former victim. For the actor, it is important to note that George "Goober" Whirmer is totally ignorant of the fact that his behavior is abnormal. He sees himself as cool, sexy, a man irresistible to women. The audience, on the other hand, perceives him as a harassing, narcissistic "know-it-all." Here's the start of the interview:

SHE How do you do, Mr. *Whi*rmer. (*She over-pronounces his last name whenever possible.*) Please be seated.

HE I'm super, just super. Nice to meet you, Miss … uh …

SHE Birdock.

HE Birdock. That's a nice name. You can really wrap your tongue around that one. (*They laugh.*)

SHE Unlike Whirmer.

HE Well, you know what they say.

SHE What's that.

HE The early birdock …

BOTH … catches the whirmer.

SHE Oh, that's very funny.

HE I'm a funny man.

SHE You certainly are, Mr. Whirmer.

HE Is your boss in?

SHE I beg your pardon?

HE Mr. … uh … (*He consults a card.*) Rosetti.

SHE (*laughing*)   Oh.

HE What's so funny?

SHE *I'll* be interviewing you, Mr. Whirmer.

HE Oh.

SHE Does that bother you?

HE Hmmm?

SHE My interviewing you. Does that bother you?

HE Not at all, not at all.

SHE You seem upset.

HE Why should I be upset?

SHE Well, I just thought …

HE With a beautiful woman like you asking me questions?

SHE Why, thank you. Now …

HE I just thought I might be seeing the boss, that's all.

SHE He's very busy.

HE I see, I see.

SHE Are you all right?

HE Yes, I'm perfectly fine.

SHE Now it says here on your resume . . .

HE Are you married?[20]

(Act Two)

For the play to be really funny, the actor playing Whirmer, while grounding his characterization in human truth, needs to amplify his arrogance and sleaziness so that the audience will be eager for his downfall. The actor can increase Goober's sense of overblown self-importance by experimenting with various behaviors and mannerisms; for instance, a preoccupation with his hair, constantly touching and arranging it. He thinks he is uncommonly handsome and preens himself, fluffing out wrinkles in his jacket, fussily picking off lint, and so on.

When she says, "I'll be interviewing you, Mr. Whirmer," he has to appear visibly disturbed that he will not be meeting with the boss who he had, of course, assumed was a man. When she notices his reaction and asks if her gender bothers him, he deals with Ms. Birdock the only way he knows how, by sexualizing her: "Why should I be upset . . . With a beautiful woman like you asking me questions." But we know that she is way ahead of him, having set up the whole sham interview. Trying to make her forget his earlier display of irritation, he now flirts more seriously. When she tries to bring the conversation back to nonsexual matters with "Now let's not beat around the bush," he leers at her with his, "To coin a phrase."[21] These frantic attempts to maintain or even enhance his image, these improvisations in response to a woman's superior wit and logic are funny—doubly so, as we know they are self-inflicted. The degree to which the actor convinces us that Goober is entirely ignorant of his being a sleazebag is one of the factors that will make a huge difference in how funny the audience finds his character, and the play.

After patronizing his advances with a little laugh, she lures him into talking about the only legitimate topic: whether or not he's right for the position. He claims he was not "fired" from his last job but "let go"; she asks him why:

HE Ethics.
SHE Oh.
HE The boss's daughter, moving up.
SHE Uh-huh.
HE I wouldn't stand for it. I spoke my mind.
SHE Good for you.
HE I always speak my mind.
SHE So do I.
HE Don't get me wrong. I admire a good businesswoman more than you do . . .
SHE I'm sure you do. (*They laugh.*)
HE . . . but this girl was a nincompoop.
SHE That's just awful.[22]

(Act Two)

Completely oblivious that his misogyny is exposed, he is no less ignorant of how much his interview performance is failing.

She lets him rave on before interrupting him with the kind of objectifying comment that he would likely have made if he were in power: "You have very nice eyes."[23] Surprised and delighted by her boldness, Goober falls deeper into her trap: he starts to flirt even more intensely. The cuter he tries to be, the funnier it is. When she asks, "What qualifies you, Goober, above anyone else for this job?" he replies with absolute conviction, "Well, I'm . . . uh . . . (*Silence*) . . . I'm sexy."[24] When she confronts him with the fact that he is married, he repugnantly replies, "We all make mistakes."[25]

His line "You look very familiar"[26] needs somehow to be "framed" for the audience, as it provides a clue as to what will now transpire between the two. Realizing that he's starting to recognize her, she knows she has to speed up his humiliation, and therefore goes right for his weak spot: "What do you feel about working for a woman, Goober?"[27] He doesn't understand what she's talking about until she reveals that *she* is actually the boss. Humiliated, deprived of what he thought was his superior status as a male, he is now ready for her to turn the tables as she presses the assault, objectifying him further: "Stand up, Goober. (*He does.*) Walk away from me. (*He does so, hesitatingly.*) Now turn around. (*He faces her.*) All the way. And take off your coat and tie."[28] Her aim here is to make him to feel the same way that she felt when he first met her. While he is undressing, she keeps the pressure on, attacking his sense of importance: Can he type? At what speed? Initially, he thinks she is joking: "Forty words a minute. But I'm improving."[29] When she sweetens the deal, offering six hundred dollars a week in salary, he discovers that the raise will be for "services rendered."[30] Next, she further reduces the exchange to an appraisal of simply his physical attributes: "Come over and sit down. (*He does*.) Now cross your legs. (*He does.*) Uncross them."[31]

This is a critical moment in her plan: if he refuses, the pleasure in her payback would essentially be over. So, when he says, "Yes, I *would* mind," she has to sweeten the deal further, offering him seven hundred a week "under the table."[32] The victim's comedy takes one more turn. She knows his weaknesses: sex and money. She entices Goober to stand and to unbutton his shirt. Then he strips down to his bikini briefs. He starts gyrating his pelvis, making himself into a spectacle. It is at this moment, with him almost naked and writhing on the floor, that she puts the finishing touches on her revenge. Crossing back behind the desk, she assumes a much more business-like tone: "Now what would you do for a thousand?"[33]

After a few more twists and turns in the negotiations and the humiliations, she reveals herself as Stella Whipple, his secretary for two weeks in 1975, the one who was fired when she "wouldn't ..." (a word they bandy about three times). She then offers to hire him, as he clings desperately to his "pride."

A shift in status, a collapse of dignity, and self-ignorance are essential to Pielmeier's comedy here. They create a separation, a gap in empathy, where the humor lies, and they are crucial to creating the dramatic irony that makes an audience's superior attitude toward the character possible.

"Where We Went Wrong Was Getting on a Boat"

Comedy is often driven by plot, with characters struggling under the heavy hand of fate. Even if their wills, desires, or conscious objective seem to determine what happens, the fact remains that there are elements in their physiological makeup—what the Elizabethans would call their "humors"—that are beyond their control. Once exposed, characters in romantic comedies may see themselves or others in a new light, and realize they have been fools and not who they thought they were.

Or they may not, for ignorance can enhance the comedy. Guildenstern, the self-professed, often pompous pseudo-intellectual of Tom Stoppard's play *Rosencrantz and Guildenstern Are Dead*, thinks he can trace everything that has happened to them to a single decision, a moment in time: their getting on a boat. He celebrates human will, or, to be more accurate, *his* will. If, at the start of the play, he can't explain adequately why the coins keep coming up heads, he now thinks that, in the face of the courtiers' own impending doom, he has the answer: getting on a boat. Guildenstern remains oblivious of the larger forces, almost all of which are beyond his control, sealing his fate and that of Rosencrantz as well. And this ignorance is inseparable from a lack of knowledge about himself.

A comic character like Guildenstern is perpetually ignorant of himself on at least two levels, imagining, first, that "he" determines his own fate, and, second, that the way he is doing things is the best way to do them. The only way to play this character is with the attitude that he's right and the world is wrong. He has to have absolute confidence in the correctness of his actions, of his judgment in any situation. The more certain the character is, the funnier his situation becomes. Regarding the necessary ignorance of the comedic character, Henri Bergson observed:

> Take any other comic character. However conscious he may be of what he says and does, if he is comic it is because there is an aspect of himself which he ignores, a side which escapes him: it is because of that alone that he will make us laugh.[34]

Generally, comedy embodies a "lighter" view of our world, with its usual focus on the everyday, on men and women who are less than noble, on human foibles rather than deep-seated depravity, on ethical issues short of crimes against humanity. Our persistent bit of advice to actors in comedy has been to approach your character's needs with a serious attempt to satisfy them—especially if those needs are based on ignorance or a false sense of importance. Resist the urge to "play the laugh" but instead play your character's objectives. Always ground comedic characters in a recognizable human reality, however silly or absurd the circumstances (or the characters) may at first appear.

Take the comedy in which you are featured, the play, seriously—as something of substance, something more than "entertainment" in the most limited sense of that word, something demanding the same high standards of acting as the grandest tragedy. Take it seriously so that the audience doesn't.

* * *

Chapters 3 and 4 examined the "craft" of comedy acting for theatre. What do you find comic in your character and, finding that, how do you make the character "real," bring him or her to life, even if just for the two hours' traffic of the stage? How does the actor collaborate with the playwright in establishing a comic world inhabited by characters who make the audience laugh? It is as simple and as profound, as challenging as that. It is, in a word, a *craft* that complements the playwright's *art* and that of the genre comedy. Here, we invoke once again the two essential words in this book's subtitle.

Chapter 5 addresses the broader psychological and performance issues an actor will come by in playing comedy, focusing on the perception of "obstacles" or whatever it is the comic character must overcome. His objective, informing what he says and what he does, will be to overcome that obstacle. An obstacle that may seem trivial, unworthy, absurd, ill-informed, or just plain crazy to us, the audience, does not appear so to the comic character. Correspondingly, whatever the actor may think about it in real life, onstage, he must take that obstacle as seriously as does his character. Indeed, the disparity between the character's attitude and that of the audience, as well as that of the actor outside the play, is the basis for comedy. But, what if a comedy blurs that disparity? What happens if a character's obstacle and his objective in overcoming it remind us of ostensibly more serious, more real obstacles that we face in our own lives? What if we see something of ourselves—maybe even a good bit of ourselves—in the comic character? And, if this happens, does our laughter become self-reflective? This parabolic curve from actor to character to an audience at length identifying with the character frames Chapter 5's discussion of psychological and performance issues. What's more, we evaluate them with reference to two very different plays: David Lindsay-Abaire's

Wonder of the World, where Niagara Falls becomes a collecting ground for lost souls, and Harold Pinter's review piece *Last to Go*, in which two old men seem to babble about nothing, yet all the while there is something darker, more serious just beneath the surface of the dialogue.

Notes

1 Christopher Durang, *Beyond Therapy* (New York: Samuel French, 1983), 95.
2 John Lahr, *Prick Up Your Ears: The Biography of Joe Orton*
(New York: Knopf, distributed by Random House, 1978), 130, cited in
Durang, Author's Notes, *Beyond Therapy*, 83.
3 Durang, *Beyond Therapy*, 7–8, 10.
4 Doug Moston, *Coming to Terms with Acting: An Instructive Glossary*
(New York: Drama Book Publishers, 1993), 31.
5 Lajos Egri, *The Art of Dramatic Writing: Its Basis in the Creative
Interpretation of Human Motives* (New York: Simon & Schuster, 1946), 65.
6 Michael Shurtleff, *Audition: Everything an Actor Needs to Know to Get the
Part* (New York: Walker, 1978), 78.
7 Durang, Author's Notes, *Beyond Therapy*, 88.
8 Ron Cameron, *Acting Skills for Life* (Toronto: Simon & Pierre, 1989), 284.
9 Henri Szeps, *All in Good Timing: A Personal Account of What an Actor
Does* (Sydney: Currency Press, 1996), 5.
10 Ibid., 117.
11 Durang, Author's Notes, *Beyond Therapy*, 85.
12 Shurtleff, *Audition*, 208.
13 Maria Aitken, *Style: Acting in High Comedy* (New York: Applause Books,
1996), 111.
14 Szeps, *All in Good Timing*, 20.
15 John Pielmeier, "Cheek to Cheek," in *Impassioned Embraces*
(New York: Dramatists Play Service, 1989). Directed by Brian Rhinehart.
Circle in the Square Downtown (Bleecker Street), New York: Courage
Productions, 2000.
16 Pielmeier, "Cheek to Cheek," 32–3.
17 Ibid., 33.
18 John Pielmeier, "Goober's Descent," in *Impassioned Embraces*
(New York: Dramatists Play Service, 1989). Directed by Brian Rhinehart.
Circle in the Square Downtown (Bleecker Street), New York: Courage
Productions, 2000.
19 Pielmeier, "Goober's Descent," 93.
20 Ibid., 87–8.
21 Ibid., 88.
22 Ibid., 88–9.

23   Ibid., 89.
24   Ibid.
25   Ibid., 90.
26   Ibid.
27   Ibid.
28   Ibid.
29   Ibid.
30   Ibid., 91.
31   Ibid.
32   Ibid.
33   Ibid., 92.
34   Henri Bergson, "Laughter," trans. Arlin Hiken Armstrong, in *Dramatic Theory and Criticism: Greeks to Grotowski*, ed. Bernard F. Dukore (New York: Holt, Rinehart and Winston, 1974), 744.

5

PSYCHOLOGICAL AND PERFORMANCE ISSUES IN PLAYING COMEDY

In Chapter 3, we spoke of the character's objective and how he must pursue it passionately, almost exclusively to anything else—as if his life depended in it. Here, we examine the larger issues, the underpinnings, behind these objectives. We return to obstacles, this time within a broader context, because they are at the very center of what constitutes comedy—and so ought to be the main focus of the comic actor. To this end, we will look at two very different plays: David Lindsay-Abaire's *Wonder of the World*[1] and Harold Pinter's review sketch, *Last to Go*.[2]

Energy and Intensity

When energy or intensity is missing onstage, the audience cannot feel the urgency with which the characters must pursue their objectives. Sometimes a director will tell an actor his performance lacks energy or that the actor needs to restore the intensity he showed during rehearsals or has lost after many performances. But the words "energy" and "intensity" themselves can seem vague or amorphous—unless looked at in terms of what the character needs.

A formula, then: energy = intensity of need. It is axiomatic to say that most characters *need* to change other characters in some way. But if what the character says is not perceived as an effort to overcome obstacles, the audience will lose interest. Urgency of need must be behind every action and each word that is spoken. By making the stakes as high as possible, the actor increases the weight and import of his language and keeps the audience focused on what his character needs.

"I need more energy from you" doesn't mean increase the volume, as one can be just as intense with a whisper as with a scream, and it certainly doesn't mean increase the speed, as slowing down and punctuating each word often creates a highly dramatic and compelling moment onstage. So what the director really means by "more intensity" is that you should raise the emotional stakes. "If I do not get this job, I'm going to kill myself." Again that formula, energy = intensity of need.

Maria Aitken has spoken of an "immediacy" that gives comedy a sense of "heightened realism." In *Style: Acting in High Comedy*, she asserted that "what grabs an audience's attention is immediacy. This is achieved by concentration, and ... the concentration of the actor lures the concentration of the audience."[3] For characters in comedy, situations are seldom trivial or inconsequential, however much they may appear to be so.

As directors, we too often see actors choose passive, unspecified objectives for their characters. When working on your character, always try to think of needs as active and aggressive verbs, rather than as passive nouns. To raise the stakes and therefore the tension level of a scene, it often becomes necessary to amplify your needs, to blow them up to an almost exaggerated level. For example, your need should not be just "to be a success" but "to conquer the world," not only "to make her love me" but "to woo her, again and again." Here are a few further examples:

Noun	Verb
I want wealth.	I must own the world.
I want love.	I must seduce, overwhelm.
I want attention.	I must fascinate, dazzle.

The actor should *never* think in terms of emotional states of being, but what the character needs. In this regard, character is not what you are but what you want; thus:

Adjective	Verb
I am angry.	I must crush, destroy, eliminate.
I am happy.	I must show you how happy I am.
I am drunk.	I must convince, assure you that I am sober.

Broadway actor and chair of the Actors Studio Drama School Andreas Manolikakis has said that "comedy is extreme behavior which expresses the deepest internal need."[4] Almost every theorist of comedy says the same thing: always make the stakes life or death. That is what holds the audience's interest.

One of the best definitions of acting comes from David Ball's *Backwards and Forwards: A Technical Manual for Reading Plays*: "You do not really know a play until you see how every word is intended by its speaker to overcome some obstacle to getting what he wants."[5] For acting coach and author Michael Shurtleff, "In comedy the needs in the relationship must be even greater than they are in drama, the competition is keener and more immediate, the game-playing is for life and death stakes every move of the way."[6]

Wonder of the World

There may be no better example of a comedy demanding energy and nonstop intensity, let alone game-playing for life-and-death stakes, than David Lindsay-Abaire's *Wonder of the World*. The plot revolves around the journey of a middle-class woman from Brooklyn to Niagara Falls. She leaves her sexually objectionable husband and her bland, sedate life for one of thrills and excitement in one of the most romantic places on earth. Along the way, she meets a colorful cast of characters: an alcoholic determined to commit suicide, a handsome but tragic boat captain, a pair of oddball private detectives, and the McShane sextuplets—five characters played by the same actress.

In this excerpt, Cass, searching for a new life without her husband Kip, meets Lois, who wants to end her life by plummeting over Niagara Falls in a barrel:

Lois *I* was abandoned.
Cass Wow. Like the Lindbergh baby.
Lois The Lindbergh baby was kidnapped, not abandoned.
Cass Or so the authorities would have us believe.
Lois You're weird.
Cass Who abandoned you?
Lois My husband. I came home to an empty house and a note which said I was a bad person because I drank too much and crashed cars.

Cass Hey, *I* almost left a note. But my husband came home
    for lunch.

Lois Good thing. A note is a terrible thing to come home to.
    I know. The bastard. Ah, fuck him. (*Swigs at a flask.*)

Cass You ever been to The Falls?

Lois Just once. A million years ago. We called it a honeymoon.

Cass Uh-huh. And what's this on your lap?

Lois It's my revenge.

Cass I see. Is it a bomb of some kind?

Lois No. A bomb?

Cass I was guessing.

Lois (*removes blanket from a large barrel*) Ta-da.

Cass Look at that. It's a … big barrel.

Lois Heavy too. My legs fell asleep thirty miles ago. I can't move.
    That's okay. I always wanted to know what it would feel like to
    be a paraplegic.

Cass My father's a paraplegic.

Lois I'm sorry. Did I offend you?

Cass No. I was just thinking that I have his phone number if you
    have any other questions about what it feels like. (*Beat.*) So.
    A barrel, huh? You gonna hit him with it?

Lois *Hit* him with it?

Cass Again, I'm just guessing here.

Lois Niagara Falls? … A *barrel*?

Cass Ohhhhh … You're gonna go to *Niagara Falls* with a *barrel*.

Lois Right.

Cass To get your revenge.

Lois Exactly.

Cass Are you gonna hide in it, and then jump out and scare him?

Lois Are you a moron?

Cass If I had a nickel for every—

Lois I'm going to go over The Falls.

Cass (*realizing*)   Ahhhhh … But you'll die.

Lois Ay, there's the rub.

Cass The rub?

Lois Imagine it. Poor Lois bobbing up and down at the bottom of
    The Falls, surrounded by bits and pieces of a smashed pickle
    barrel.

Cass It's a pickle barrel?

Lois Ted loves pickles. See, that'll add to the power of it all.

Cass It's funny, isn't it? I'm starting my new life. You're
ending yours.

Lois That's *funny* to you?

Cass Well not funny so much as— (*interrupts herself*) Hey, do you
wanna be my sidekick?[7]

(Act One, Scene Two)

Abandonment by a husband leading, in one instance, to a search for
a new life; in the other, suicide. A new life and suicide—these are the
needs of the two characters, serious objectives requiring the "intensity
of need" we spoke about earlier. But how serious is either character in
their choice? Cass will produce a list of all the things she's planning to
experience now that she's free of her husband. Lois has a list, but with
just one item: she'll plunge to her death going over the falls in a barrel.
A list, a barrel—a little out of the ordinary, but not that much, and so,
once the actor establishes this "normal" choice for each character, for
whom the goal is not trivial or inconsequential, the challenge becomes
how to best incorporate the humor. Here, in this bizarre situation, these
fairly improbable circumstances, is where the actor's spirit of play
comes in!

What do you do with Lois's correction that the Lindbergh baby was
"kidnapped," not "abandoned"? Cass apologizes for not leaving her
husband a note, as Lois's husband did, with the excuse that he came
home from lunch unexpectedly. Does the humor of the apology undercut
whatever grief she feels at being abandoned? When Lois jokes that
moving the heavy barrel only encourages her to know what it's like to be
a paraplegic, is Cass serious or sarcastic in offering to introduce her to
her paraplegic father? Lois revels in the fact that a pickle barrel will only
remind Ted of his favorite food—isn't taking her life enough to define
her revenge? Again, the actors need to think not so much of what the
characters are, but of what they want.

If such humor is not to be freestanding, extraneous to the recognizable
human truths of Cass and Lois, then it is crucial for the actor to make
these jokes intrinsic to the situation, at one with the character in question.
Does their inability to stay focused, to remain serious, only show that
both women are not as fully committed to their objects as they profess?

Like magnets, they bond over their similarities (both are at odds with their husbands) as much as their differences. (As Cass says, "It's funny, isn't? I'm starting my new life. You're ending yours.") Does this budding friendship trump the past history each brings to the encounter?

Perhaps Cass is genuinely given to conspiracy theories. And Lois's seeming despair only thinly hides her need to stay alive and enact a pictorial revenge on Ted as she imagines herself "bobbing up and down at the bottom of the falls, surrounded by bits and pieces of a smashed pickle barrel." The actors will, of course, know the full arc of their character—so, how do you play characters who might be unaware of how defensive their humor can be and what it is hiding? Cass and Lois are deadly serious about objectives we take as comic, even absurd. The more the actors amplify their characters' needs, the funnier they will appear to their audience. At the same time, to underscore their budding friendship the actors need to find an emotional subtext for each that complements, perhaps in ways duplicates, that of the other.

The following scene from *Wonder* seems built around an old shaggy dog story, the crazy circumstances of the death of Captain Mike's wife. That's joke A, and joke B is the source of the flirtation between Mike and Cass.

Captain Mike *I* was married once.

Cass Were you?

Captain Mike Her name was Dinah. She had a cotton candy cart up by the wax museum. The sweetest woman alive. We met bowling. Her hair was all up in this lump, with a pencil holding it together. You ever see that?

Cass Sure.

Captain Mike I used to call her Lumpy. It was a nickname.

Cass Cute.

Captain Mike Yeah, she was something.

Cass Until she turned on you, right? Until she transformed into a grotesque stranger?

Captain Mike No, that never happened.

Cass Oh. I assumed because you said "*was*" married.

Captain Mike No, we ... uh ... oh, never mind.

Cass No, go ahead.

Captain Mike Well, you know those wholesale warehouse stores? You become a member and get huge amounts of food for pennies?

Cass *Love* the Costco. You can buy a twenty-pound bag of Cheetos for four dollars.

Captain Mike Exactly. Well, I enjoyed shopping at Costco, but Dinah thought it was silly. Said the food was just too darn big.

Cass So you divorced?

Captain Mike No. I came home late from The Falls one night, and the house was so quiet. Like cathedral quiet. Has your house ever been so quiet you thought you might stop breathing?

Cass Yes. I've lived with that for years.

Captain Mike And I go to the kitchen and Dinah is lying on the floor and there's a restaurant-sized four-gallon jar of peanut butter smeared across the tiles. She was apparently putting the jar away—it was kept on one of the higher shelves—and she lost her grip, and the peanut butter plummeted and smashed against her forehead. The coroner said that the weight of the blow could've killed a gorilla. She died nearly instantly.

Cass My goodness.

Captain Mike I don't know why I was so stubborn. We didn't need all that peanut butter. A small jar would've been plenty. She must've gotten hungry waiting for me. And the thing is, I stopped to rent a video on the way home. And I think if I had just been a little earlier, or if I hadn't stopped for the video, maybe she wouldn't have reached for that gargantuan jar.

Cass What video was it?

Captain Mike What?

Cass What video? What'd you rent?

Captain Mike Uh ... I think it was *Caddyshack*.

Cass Oh, that's good. That's a good movie.

Captain Mike I guess.

Cass Sure. With the gopher and everything? That's funny.

Captain Mike Well, I didn't actually get to watch it.

Cass Oh, that's right. I'm sorry. Oh my god, I'm so sorry. My husband's right, I'm such a scatterbrain.

Captain Mike Husband?[8]

(Act One, Scene Six)

This comic exchange is enhanced by the physical choices the actors make—gestures, facial expressions, positions on stage—and, of course, is equally influenced by what their partner does. To help the actors connect—in this case, both physically and through sounds—we used an acting game called "Pass around." Requiring at least three players, the object is to duplicate the rhythm of the person next to you. One person starts, and, either by tapping out a rhythm with the hands, voice, or both, "passes" that rhythm along, until the rhythm makes its way back to the originator. The more complicated the rhythm, the funnier and better—say, a combination of intricate claps and crazy sounds. There are no winners or losers here; everyone tries to do his or her part in keeping up the exact rhythm with which the round started. We find this exercise helps the actors tune into each other, by requiring a tight focus on repetition and mimicry.

At first, these characters are re-separated by the tragic death of Mike's wife, with Cass and the captain remaining a discreet distance from each other, their faces polite masks. If they check each other out with their eyes, such "exploration" is seen only by the audience, who get to enjoy the game of eyes being averted a split second before being detected. Here, even though the circumstances of the captain's wife's death are absurd, the comedy arouses pity rather than fear for the grieving husband—or the dead wife, for that matter.

And, in stage two, the pity aroused in his audience of one onstage brings the two closer, Cass out of a mother-like sympathy, Mike finding someone with whom to share his story. They get close, emotionally, physically. The moment Cass learns the captain was "married once," she tries but can't hide the fact that she's attracted. She gives the captain an enticing smile, brushes her hair back seductively, but, not knowing the tragedy behind "married once," only manages to confuse him. In a sense, he's still "married" to his wife, and quickly moves away from Cass, perhaps moments before she puts a would-be friendly hand on his shoulder. Cass will not be denied, and crosses to join him downstage. She is a foot from him, and he moves again, although perhaps not as far this time. He's becoming interested in this woman, bolder. Meanwhile, the actor must appear at cross-purposes, attending to the loving memories of a dead wife in addition to the growing attraction to this new woman. As a defense against what he feels inside, he launches into praise of Lumpy. Discouraged as he strolls down memory lane, Cass, embarrassed, takes a step back, trying to regain that formal, disinterested pose of the start of their meeting.

In the short third stage, they separate once when the captain hears the word "husband."

So, here they are, two people abandoned by their mates (through death or literal abandonment), married (in memory, legally) but not "married" in the most optimistic construction of the word. They need each other.

If the actor is self-confident, maintaining a distance from his character, at one with a state of relaxation, he can play two contrasting states of mind as the captain recounts the weird circumstances of Lumpy's death. Is he at all aware that he is melodramatically tragic? That is, does the actor play Mike as exhibiting real grief, or is he exaggerating that grief as a way of attracting the sympathy of this woman alive, next to him—a woman he finds attractive? Let's not forget what a simple gesture like her hand touching his might do to this equation. As he blames himself for what happened that fatal night, for his wife's death by an oversized jar of peanut butter, does the captain shrink into himself, trying to ward off his guilt? If he does, does this turn Cass on even more? How does she try to hide from him her joy at the "good news" of Lumpy's death? Does she find this silly attempt to blame himself rather appealing? Is Mike a man with a sense of responsibility Kip never had?

Talk about rapid changes in emotion: here, in the middle of Mike's eulogy, she asks, "What video was that?" Is this a deliberate tactic? A way of changing the subject—enough of Lumpy! Or, does the actor build here on Cass's comic inability to focus, which we saw in the previous scene? What need does this digression serve for each character? This time, she almost succeeds in dragging him out of the past, but then he sinks again into his memories. But notice how the digression evaporates in stages: Mike reminds both of them, but mostly himself, that he didn't get to watch the movie. She apologizes as they draw apart, and then he pulls further apart when her self-deprecating apology—her husband had called her a "scatterbrain"—backfires. The characters are full of anxiety here: Mike wanting to escape the past, even as he relives his days with Lumpy; Cass finding herself in competition with a dead woman for a very-much-alive man. The characters are full of anxiety, yet the actors aren't—they are in control, and this fact will be reassuring to the audience. Jealousy, escaping the past ... we may know them, but, along with the actors, we are experiencing these common human emotions at a distance, through the comedy. Note too, though, that such distance doesn't need to go as far as that icily unemotional stance that Denis Diderot's "paradox," discussed below, would place on the actor.[9]

We laugh at the sudden shift of emotions—good-bye Kip and Lumpy—because the characters find what is happening between them perfectly natural. Death and lust—the former reduced to the comic, the latter kindled by a deep need and mutual interest. The link between the two is established.

Later, in the next act, as the barrel carrying Cass and Lois moves wildly through the water, the physical action will present quite a challenge for the two actors. But they must also link the physical action onstage with the absurd dialogue that accompanies it.

> *The current picks up dramatically. The barrel pitches. The women scream.*
>
> **Cass** and **Lois**   Whoaaaaa.
>
> **Lois** (*to the heavens*)   Okay, you win! (*Tosses her flask in the river.*) No more booze!
>
> **Cass**   Why'd you do that?!
>
> **Lois**   I've stopped drinking!
>
> **Cass**   You can't stop drinking, you're an alcoholic!
>
> **Lois**   Well. I'm turning over a new leaf!
>
> **Cass**   Yeah, it doesn't really work like that!
>
> **Lois** (*back out front*)   I can see the edge!
>
> **Cass**   At least I'll get my answer!
>
> **Lois**   Heeelp!
>
> **Cass**   They'll either pull us out of the water in pieces or as whole and perfect as newborn babies!
>
> **Lois**   Hold on!
>
> **Cass**   But whatever happens, the result will be unmistakable!
>
> **Lois**   Here it comes. Here it comes. Here it—! (*Suddenly there's a thud. The barrel stops. The women jerk forward. The waterfall is still roaring, but the barrel has stopped moving. They look around, confused.*)
>
> **Cass**   Well, hell's bells.
>
> **Lois**   What happened?!
>
> **Cass**   We stopped!
>
> **Lois**   How come?!

Cass We're stuck!

Lois Stuck?!

Cass On a big rock!

Lois Oh! (*They both look around. Odd.*)

Cass Does this seem strange to you?!

Lois Compared to *what*?!

Cass It doesn't seem odd that we didn't go over?!

Lois Not really, no!

Cass It's like this boulder was *waiting* for us!

Lois Please don't jostle the barrel!

Cass Maybe this is my answer! Maybe this is the hand of God Captain Mike was talking about!

Lois Or maybe it's just a rock!

Cass *considers this. Everything seems to drain out of her.*

Cass Right.

Lois Heeeeeeeeeelp! (*Looks over the edge.*) It's a long way down isn't it?! (*Calls again.*) Someone heeeeeeelp!

Cass (*pause*)   When does the clarity come?

Lois (*beat*)   Do you see that? (*Points DSR.*)

Cass The sun?

Lois Yes. It came up. And you're breathing. What else do you want?

Cass *has no response.* **Lois** *has made a good point. Something changes.*

Cass Some breakfast would be nice. (*Pause, and then points DSL.*) What are those gardens?

Lois That's Canada.

Cass Oh. It really *is* prettier on that side.

Lois Yes it is. Maybe we can have breakfast over there.

Cass I'd like that.

They look around, taking in the whole panorama as if for the first time. They breathe easily.

Cass It's a nice view.

Lois That's true.

The women stay in the barrel, taking in the view. The overwhelming roar of The Falls rises as the lights slowly fade.[10]

(Act Two, Scene Four)

As the barrel moves through the water, the action unfolds in five distinct stages that serve as guideposts for the actors, allowing them to build on and hence adjust to the growing bond between two characters who, at the start of the play, were so separated emotionally and psychologically. Each stage plays a clear variation on the unfolding comedy leading to resolution, completion.

In stage one, as the *"current picks up dramatically"* and the barrel *"pitches,"* the two women become discrete personalities as they assess what is happening. Does Lois cry "No more booze" in the hope that the vow will make her worth saving? Why is Cass the cynical one about her partner's bargain with fate: "Yeah, it doesn't really work like that"? After all, at the start of the play, she was going to lead a new life, not take her life. The actors might want to consider if the two characters have exchanged personalities. Physically confined to the same barrel, they themselves seem to be on different stages. They hug each other in their mutual terror, but then separate physically, as far as the set will allow them. Are they addressing some unseen force, locating it in the audience? If so, what change in delivery might this option dictate?

Then, in stage two, Lois keeps her eyes on the current, their present predicament, calling out for "Heeeeeelp!" just in case someone is nearby, while Cass philosophizes on their fate, being either death or salvation, before concluding that, whatever happens, "the result will be mistakable." Now the bonding established earlier in the play is coming apart. Again, how might the actors in their delivery, in their gestures, underscore this split?

In stage three, the *"thud"* draws the women together, as if they were a single character, their lines running into each other's, with Lois's question "What happened?" answered by Cass's "We're stuck," and Lois's "Stuck?!" leading to Cass's "On a big rock." They cling to each other, faces pressed together, as if one could just as easily speak for the other. If they had individual styles of delivery in the previous section, how might they mirror each other here in tone, rhythm, emphasis? Might they try, in rehearsal, Chapter 2's "Mirror" acting exercise, in which one actor duplicates the movements or voice of the other?

In stage four, when *"they both look around,"* Cass reverts to her old self, trying to analyze this "strange" situation, while Lois is predictably literal, non-theological: for her, it's a rock and not God at work. For the actor, why does practical assessment seem to drain everything out of Cass, who now agrees? After her final cry "When does the clarity come?" she and her partner focus on what is there before them—real, not theoretical: they see the sun. The actor playing Lois is dominant here, the comic duo momentarily unbalanced. Again, how can the actor playing Cass imitate the tone, style, or speech patterns of her fellow actor?

In stage five, the final section, the comic situation resolves itself as the women draw closer. Convincing Cass that that both are alive, "breathing," Lois asks plaintively, "What else do you want?" This time, Cass gives the practical, mundane answer: "Breakfast." If this were music, the final section would be played *legato*. How can the actors make their performance here distinctive, with a sustained tone and subtext we have not heard so clearly before? The five stages, distinct and yet linked, present a challenge for the actors, requiring that energy and intensity, refreshed night after night, that we discussed at the start of this chapter.

The "arc" of comedy, the development of the character over the course of the play, is shown here as the two actors have moved from those frantic, self-absorbed positions and distinct styles of delivery to the physical and verbal finally enacting the generic resolution of comedy, which is expressed sometimes by a feast or a dance, a coda signifying that all is well, and the comically absurd passions, the bizarre obstacles confronted earlier, are now spent, dissipated.

The Comic Actor and the Life Beyond the Play

Overcoming obstacles, making the jokes integral to the characters, connecting as actors, and playing the character's physical actions apply equally to any of the five scenes from *Wonder of the World*. Considering a well-made scene as a miniature play, with its own short "acts," is at one with taking the larger play as something whole, organic. A laugh at a particular moment, funny line, or situation is never isolated, but contributes to the pattern of ongoing response from the audience. And in that pattern is a parallel, however illusory the source, to that larger life the audience will know when exiting the theatre. In this way, the final scene of *Wonder of the World* endorses the significance of the present comedy and comedy as a genre.

Consider the miraculous moment when Janie, the marriage counselor, produces the watch that Lois lost years ago, that loss leading to the end of her marriage to Ted:

Janie Wait, there's one more thing. I'd like to finish my inspirational story.

Cass It really isn't necessary, we—

Janie So there I was, at the base of The Falls, all hope lost, about to jump overboard, when something inexplicably wonderful happened. I looked up. And in that moment, I saw something falling towards me.

Lois Was it a lady?

Janie No, it was smaller than a lady. I cupped my hands, like this, and it landed there, a sign from the Heavens. It was this very watch (*shows her watch*) inscribed with the words "Love Always." And I thought "Well, that's the answer I've been looking for." Love Always. And that answer seemed to cancel out all the bad stuff that had come before it. And I went home, and reconciled with Gary, and I've spent the rest of my life helping other couples reconnect with *their* love. Because no matter how lost everything seems, there's always room for a miracle.

Lois That's my watch.

Janie Huh? What?

Lois I dropped it and my marriage turned to shit! That's *my* watch!

Janie No, this is a sign from the heavens.

Lois It was a honeymoon present.

Cass She's right. She told me about it. That's her watch.

Janie Well … Tough shit, you're not getting it back now.

Lois *pulls out the gun and points it at* **Janie**.

Lois Gimme the watch! It's mine!

Janie *Jesus!* What are you? I am trying to *help* you people. (*Hands over the watch.*) Shame on you.

Karla This is why I love group therapy.

Lois (*looking at watch*)   It still works.

Glen Must be a Timex.

Lois Do you know what this means?

Janie Means I need a new watch.

Lois God is giving me a good shake. He's sayin' "Look lady, you got time left! Your watch ain't busted yet!" Wait'll I tell Ted! (*Rushes to the phone and dials.*)

Janie My sister pulled a gun on me once. She's a big alky too.

Karla I didn't know you had a sister.

Janie I have five sisters. We're identical. Ever hear of the McShane Sextuplets? We were on the cover of *Life* magazine. We spent our childhood on display in a petting zoo. It was an awful way to grow up, gawked at, exploited, fondled by other children. Damn my father and that contract. But we all turned out okay. Except Barb. She went bald and developed a strange Southern accent.

Lois (*into phone*)   Hello Willy?! It's Lois! ... I'm sorry to wake you up, but I've had an epiphany! ... An *epiphany*! It's this thing and I had one! Put Ted on! And don't tell me he's not there this time.[11]

(Act Two, Scene Three)

Suddenly the scene is replete with religious references. For Janie, finding the watch is "a sign from the Heavens," the chance event that led to her dedicating her life to saving others. For Lois, the fact that the watch is still running means "God is giving [her] a good shake," an "epiphany": she decides to call Ted and reconcile with him.

But such religious references are really secondary to the more important issue: the actors have to commit themselves fully to the imaginary circumstances, and have faith that what might seem a coincidence to us, something impossible, has actually happened. For the characters, the watch, this prop, is real, lifesaving—like some religious relic.

For Janie, finding it came at the very moment she was about to take her life, and is therefore something "inexplicably wonderful." The cliché "Love Always" engraved on the back was "the answer" she had been looking for, and shortly thereafter she reconciled with her husband Gary. For her, the coincidence was not random but a "miracle." Of course, we've all found an object like this, but few see it as a symbol of grace prerequisite to a religious conversion. But, when the actors' struggles are convincing, we too momentarily believe that what they say happened actually did; against reason or good sense, we too accept the improbable. They convert us, as does that theatrical moment when something literal metamorphoses into something symbolic.

The idea of stage characters going down the falls in a barrel is funny, yet it also carries a weight beyond its immediate presence. Couple that with inane dialogue and the desperate needs of each character and the contrast almost demands laughter, especially when the actors take the comedy seriously. We know Janie and Lois are crazy, and comically so, to put so such trust in a Timex (not *even* a Rolex!), and as we identify with them, we *feel* for them. But the actors have convinced us, and it is their faith that makes the comedy shine.

Self-Confidence/Relaxation and a Spirit of Play

If an actor has stage fright, the comedy cannot work. Likewise, an actor tense in real life may play a tense character, perhaps even credibly so, but there is a danger that such a character will not mesh well with other characters, let alone give the illusion of being in the "world" of the play itself. A tense, nervous actor might engage an audience's empathic response, but may fall flat in eliciting a truly humorous response. A good comic actor is keenly aware that the purpose is to make the audience laugh, whether he is telling the jokes or is the butt of others' humor. Accordingly, it is especially important that the actor emanates a sense of confidence, a perceived relaxation, and that the audience does not sense any tension beneath the surface.

In his essay "The Paradox of Acting," Denis Diderot counseled that the actor should, at all times, maintain a tight control over his emotional state and never let himself experience the same feelings the character is experiencing.[12] Consequently, this notion that an actor can remain icily objective and unemotional while his character is in the throes of a violent emotional passion has been dubbed "Diderot's paradox" by many, including those who contend that Diderot was simply critical of the hysterical and declamatory acting styles of the eighteenth century.

The comic actor knows that when a line is greeted with laughter, he must wait until the laughter reaches its peak and starts to slide back down before delivering his next line. Like the actor in a serious play, however, the comic actor must always look at his character from the outside, utilizing the very stance of detachment that Bertolt Brecht championed. When the comic actor is confident, *relaxed*, aware of his craft, and of his audience, he directs the audience's emotional investment toward his character's circumstances rather than to his own. This sense of relaxation extends even to situations when comedic characters are under extreme duress. Whatever physical discomfort Harold Lloyd's character experiences in *Safety Last!* (1923), as he hangs precipitously from the giant town clock high above a busy city street, desperately trying to wrap his feet around the clock's minute hand, crying out for help in vain (wonderfully ironic in a silent movie), his face screwed up in abject terror, knowing that at any second he might plunge to his death, the actor Lloyd remains supremely confident in his craft—relaxed.[13] And, because we know we are watching a comedy, we laugh at his predicament, but, like the actor, remain detached from any real terror or fear that Lloyd himself might be harmed doing the stunt.

To this issue of self-confidence/relaxation, we would also add a "spirit of play." In the *Poetics* (*c*.335 BC), Aristotle observed that, with tragedy, the audience simultaneously experiences the two contradictory emotions of fear and pity, and we see this in comedy as well. Since we know the character is only an actor's impersonation, we can "pity" him while keeping our distance from the stage illusion. But when that illusion is convincing, we also experience "fear," and the sense that what is happening could happen to us hits a bit too close to home. Still, in comedy there is more pity, *much* more pity, than fear. In Chapter 5 of the *Poetics*, Aristotle hinted at the way comedy should be written and, from this, suggested why this feeling of pity is the stronger. "Comedy," he affirmed, "is ... an imitation of men who are inferior but not altogether vicious. The ludicrous is a species of ugliness ... which is not painful or injurious."[14]

Whether the character is vicious, ugly, or just plain "inferior," when the audience knows the actor is confident and relaxed, pity for the character—rising from a situation that is comic, not overly serious, let alone tragic—runs parallel to a sense of play that they share with the actor. The actor, in effect, signals to the audience that "no matter what my character may be experiencing, I'm having fun, enjoying my time here on stage, and knowing you're out there." Conversely, anxiety in the actor can create anxiety in the audience, and that anxiety usually kills the humor.

Red Skelton, the comic actor from the 1950s and one of the early stars of television, was often accused of laughing too much at his own jokes, even anticipating with his laughter the audience's response. Some critics went so far as to claim that Skelton was so much his own audience that his ego got in the way. Whether he really enjoyed his own jokes as much as his laughter would seem to indicate is uncertain, but what is clear is that behind his laughter was simultaneously a performer trying to please the crowd, almost begging for their laughter, and an audience of one to his own performance.[15] Skelton's career lasted almost a half-century—talk about self-confidence, being relaxed, and a spirit of play!

Last to Go

As you look at this short review sketch by Harold Pinter, you should ask: Where are the obstacles? What's the problem? What's to overcome? Where's the energy, the intensity? Two old guys, blue-collar workers, a barman and a newspaper seller, chew the fat. Perhaps to a sophisticated, college-educated theatre audience, their conversation might seem inconsequential—just trivial, idle talk. If we find humor in these two characters, we might rush to the conclusion that our laughter is condescending. Compared to them, Willy Loman is royalty. But, first, look at the script:

> **MAN** You was a bit busier earlier.
> **BARMAN** Ah.
> **MAN** Round about ten.
> **BARMAN** Ten, was it?
> **MAN** About then.
> *Pause.*
> I passed by here about then.
> **BARMAN** Oh yes?
> **MAN** I noticed you were doing a bit of trade.
> *Pause.*
> **BARMAN** Yes, trade was very brisk here about ten.
> **MAN** Yes, I noticed.
> *Pause.*
> I sold my last one about then. Yes. About nine forty-five.
> **BARMAN** Sold your last then, did you?
> **MAN** Yes, my last "Evening News" it was. Went about twenty
> to ten.
> *Pause.*
> **BARMAN** "Evening News," was it?
> **MAN** Yes.
> *Pause.*
> Sometimes it's the "Star" is the last to go.

BARMAN Ah.

MAN Or the . . . whatsisname.

BARMAN "Standard."

MAN Yes.

Pause.

All I had left tonight was the "Evening News."

Pause.

BARMAN Then that went, did it?

MAN Yes.

Pause.

Like a shot.

Pause.

BARMAN You didn't have any left, eh?

MAN No. Not after I sold that one.

Pause.

BARMAN It was after that you must have come by here then, was it?

MAN Yes, I come by here after that, see, after I packed up.

BARMAN You didn't stop here though, did you?

MAN When?

BARMAN I mean, you didn't stop here and have a cup of tea then, did you?

MAN What, about ten?

BARMAN Yes.

MAN No, I went up to Victoria.

BARMAN No, I thought I didn't see you.

MAN I had to go up to Victoria.

Pause.

BARMAN Yes, trade was very brisk here about then.

Pause.

MAN I went to see if I could get hold of George.

BARMAN Who?

MAN George.

Pause.

BARMAN George who?

MAN George . . . whatsisname.

BARMAN Oh.

Pause.

Did you get hold of him?

MAN No. No, I couldn't get hold of him. I couldn't locate him.

BARMAN He's not about much now, is he?

Pause.

MAN When did you last see him then?

BARMAN Oh, I haven't seen him for years.

MAN No, nor me.

Pause.

BARMAN Used to suffer very bad from arthritis.

MAN Arthritis?

BARMAN Yes.

MAN He never suffered from arthritis.

Pause.

BARMAN Suffered very bad.

Pause.

MAN Not when I knew him.

Pause.

BARMAN I think he must have left the area.

Pause.

MAN Yes, it was the "Evening News" was the last to go tonight.

BARMAN Not always the last though, is it, though?

MAN No. Oh no. I mean sometimes it's the "News." Other times it's one of the others. No way of telling beforehand. Until you've got your last one left, of course. Then you can tell which one it's going to be.

BARMAN Yes.

Pause.

MAN Oh yes.

Pause.

I think he must have left the area.[16]

They meet every night at roughly the same time, ten, after Man has sold his last paper. The conversation is always the same; inquiries about how each fared that day, perhaps boasting about the number of papers sold or customers served. This is their comfort—a pleasant chat that puts the finishing touch on a day distinguished by nothing extraordinary happening. They "cling" to a routine that, by definition, never varies. Actors have found that they have to expend energy and intensity, as well as be relaxed and see the characters with a spirit of play, on making these two old men so dull, so content with an existence many of us would find insufferably comic.

The actors here and throughout the sketch need to expend energy and intensity on dialogue that may seem inconsequential, idiosyncratic, even neurotic. This doesn't mean they should show outward signs of nervousness, desperation, or tension. Far from it, for they must cling to their routine, to these seemingly bland questions and statements, as a way of hiding what is just underneath the dialogue.

However insignificant, the predictability of both time and conversation that allowed them to hold a place in the city is in doubt. To put the situation in theatrical terms, the reference to George causes them to jump a script that so far has been established, a script for which both assumed the other was off-book.

Both now attempt to overcome this new obstacle, one more difficult than determining whether the bar was busy or which paper was the last to go. First, they return to the issue of which papers go first, the *Evening News* or the *News*. The Man even reiterates his earlier absurd statement about how one knows which paper is the last to go: "No way of telling beforehand [which is the last to go]. Until you've got your last one left, of course. Then you can tell which one it's going to be."

George is put to rest; things are back in order. Yet not quite, for the routine ends with Man, after the inevitable Pinter pause, reassuring himself and his friend that the mysterious George "must have left the area." That "must" is perhaps not as reassuring, as definite, as either would have wished.

Comic because the two characters are so insignificant; ultimately the dialogue is funny not because we laugh at their absurdity but because it is so woefully, wonderfully human, as they struggle to keep at bay the obstacles, all that threatens their routine. What is trivial to us is not so trivial to Man and Barman and this helps create the humor.

Energy, Emotion, and Performance

In his "Understanding, Sensibility, and Fire" (1750), John Hill championed the naturalistic comic acting that captures "every emotion of the heart … every species of passion that human nature is capable of being affected by."[17] For the actors, the advice of the great Russian teacher Andrius Jilinsky in his *The Joy of Acting* is timely: "You must play the most ridiculous circumstances with the same degree of concentration that you give to a serious moment."[18]

* * *

Through exploring psychological themes alongside those of performance, this chapter has shown how the comic actor should first examine the play and his character, and then increase energy and intensity to play the humor. In the next chapter, we add these insights to those offered in Chapters 2, 3, and 4—the improvs and acting games used in fashioning a character, the rules for acting comedy, and the elements of the comic character—and discuss how to apply them to a single play: in this case, Michael Frayne's *Noises Off*. What we have called the "living organism" of a comic character evolves through the entire play. There is an arc in that evolution, and, as the play moves from scene to scene, the audience begins to frame and understand the character not only as portrayed by the actor behind him but also as they themselves refashion that character in terms of their own needs, interests, and even obsessions—their own life experience. They know the character is not real, only a stage impersonation, and yet he touches on their reality—he is not an abstraction. Their laughter at his absurdities, as we have argued, is also self-reflective to a degree, so long as the actor pulls them into the comic world and they are in turn involved in the character as he overcomes obstacles and pursues his objectives. *Noises Off* is one of the finest examples of the subgenre of farce. Replete with very human characters—"types," if you will, who still might remind us of ourselves—it is also very much about the theatre, the experience of being present at a performance, here from the perspective of the actors. We are invited to enter their world backstage as well as onstage. By this means, in treating the whole comedy, we consider character analysis, issues of energy and tempo, conflict, status and "the game," and the place of the character and the concomitant role of the actor in the world of farce.

Notes

1   David Lindsay-Abaire, *Wonder of the World* (New York: Dramatist's Play Service, 2003).

2 Harold Pinter, *Last to Go*, in *Harold Pinter: Complete Works*, vol. 2 (New York: Grove Press, 1990), 245–8.

3 Maria Aitken, *Style: Acting in High Comedy* (New York: Applause Books, 1996), 42.

4 Andreas Manolikakis, in conversation with Brian Rhinehart, New York, April 9, 2007.

5 David Ball, *Backward and Forward: A Technical Manual for Reading Plays* (Carbondale, IL: Southern Illinois Press, 1983), 29.

6 Michael Shurtleff, *Audition* (New York: Bantam Book, 1978), 208.

7 Lindsay-Abaire, *Wonder of the World*, 11–12.

8 Ibid., 21–2.

9 Denis Diderot, *The Paradox of Acting*, trans. Walter Herries Pollock (Memphis, TN: General Books, 2010), 4–18. Originally published as *Paradoxe sur le comédien* (London: Chatto & Windus, 1883).

10 Lindsay-Abaire, *Wonder of the World*, 67–9.

11 Ibid., 61–2.

12 Diderot, *The Paradox of Acting*.

13 See "262-01- Lloyd on Clock" (Harold Lloyd dangling from the clock in *Safety Last!*), YouTube video, 0:17, posted by Ian Abrams, January 6, 2009, https://www.youtube.com/watch?v=Hr2aj1ibVYE (accessed July 13, 2016).

14 Aristotle, *Poetics*, in *Criticism: The Major Texts*, ed. Walter Jackson Bate (New York: Harcourt Brace & World, 1952). See also Sidnell, *Sources of Dramatic Theory*, 41.

15 See "Red Skelton Tribute, Red Skelton show, Red Skelton Show tribute Pigeon Forge," YouTube video, 4:48, posted by RedSkeleton4u, April 12, 2013, https://www.youtube.com/watch?v=8S9kU2zojs4 (accessed July 13, 2016).

16 Pinter, *Last to Go*, 245–8.

17 John Hill, "Understanding, Sensibility, and Fire," in *Actors on Acting: The Theories, Techniques, and Practices of the Great Actors of All Times as Told in Their Own Words*, ed. Toby Cole and Helen Krich Chinoy (New York: Crown Publishers, 1949), 127. See also John Hill, *The Actor: A Treatise on the Art of Playing* (London: R. Griffiths, 1750), 21.

18 Christine Edwards, *The Stanislavski Heritage: Its Contribution to the Russian and American Theatre* (New York: New York University Press, 1965), 42.

6
PLAYING THE WHOLE COMEDY

Good comic actors fashion their role on a character's progress through the play, seeing growth in terms of a through-line or "arc." For them, their character is a living organism, shaped and changed by interaction with other characters. To appraise this approach, we refer to Michael Frayn's *Noises Off*,[1] discussing a sampling of scenes in their given order. Good comedies, if they are linear, grow scene by scene, allowing the audience to experience and react to the unfolding narrative. But even if the comedy has a nonlinear design and is not driven by plot as conventionally understood, the scenes still generally progress in a meaningful order as that delineation of character or theme is revealed. (We base this inference on our experiences as both director of and actor in Frayn's very funny play.)

Noises Off

This "play in three acts" is one of the most ingenious, not to mention commercially successful, farces ever written. It has seen multiple incarnations on the West End of London, and on Broadway in New York City. Besides arguably being one of the funniest plays in the Western canon, it is also a fairly astute lampooning of commercial theatre—specifically, the ubiquity of "bedroom" farces in the 1960s and 1970s. Plays like *Don't Dress for Dinner* (1987) by Marc Camoletti, or *Who Goes Bare* (1974) by Richard Harris and Leslie Darbon, were extremely popular throughout this period. *Noises Off* also makes a lovingly critical swipe at touring theatre, which is known for hiring very new (cheaper) performers or older, nearly "washed-up" ones, all desperate to work. Frayn takes a full swing on this note in the biographies of the "players" to be included in the faux program at the beginning of the play text.

Farce is a form that pre-dates the Greeks, going back to the *Fabula Atellana* of the ancient Italians, and its form was later codified and frequently used by writers as well-known as Aristophanes, Menander, Plautus, Molière, and Shakespeare. Farce was *the* dominant form throughout the Middle Ages in France, England, and Germany, finally emerging as the *commedia dell'arte*, whose influences were and still are far-reaching, its effects being seen in the Comédie-Française, Elizabethan drama, and comedies to the present day.

Comedy tends to be intellectual, even literary, while farce is willfully absurd, highly physical, and often grotesque. In farce, plot and character are often sacrificed to the nonstop verbal and visual jokes, or the traditional rules of realistic play making, such as linear plot, progressive action, cause–effect logic. Farce bends any and all rules to get the loudest and longest laughs.

In farce, characters are generally more like puppets than fully realized naturalistic characters, but that doesn't mean that they shouldn't be portrayed and perceived as real human beings as opposed to empty caricatures. Nine out of ten characters in farces are flat, "stock" type characters, and that in itself poses an interesting challenge for the comedic actor—namely, how do you create believable "types"? How do you combine exaggeration with naturalism to create extreme yet believable characters? Farce exists on the razor's edge of too much and not enough, and nowhere is this truer than in the acting of it.

The audience will only stay interested as long as the actor continues to play the objectives, not the comedy. The character must stay focused on his obstacles and continually think about how to satisfy his character's needs, not how to satisfy the audience. The words and situations do that for themselves. Your main goal as an actor of farce is to present believable characters.

In a typical farce, the characters are easily recognizable types, with no real depth or self-awareness. The logic of the play is improbable, relying on contrivances and easy coincidences, and the comedy depends to a great deal on slapstick and broad physical humor. *Noises Off* is different, though, because it is a farce within a farce and is based on real people, so the characters have more dimensions to their personality and overall makeup than the characters of "Nothing On," the play within the play.

In the first Act One (there are three), the set is typical of "door" and "bedroom" farces: a country estate with two floors and lots of doors. The mansion is a converted posset mill and realistically and rustically furnished and decorated. The entire set then swings around and the audience can now see the backstage, bare bones, made up of unpainted timber and other construction materials. Backstage is perpetually a place of some risk, as the actors and technicians know well—heads get bumped, toes get broken. Accidents, some fatal, have occurred. This place of "danger" raises the stakes concerning all the physical action in the play, and that, coupled with near-physical violence, pratfalls, and characters swinging axes, serves to keep the tension high throughout an act in which the principal characters are silent. In the third act (i.e., the third Act One), the set has turned back around, and the audience sees, once again, the interior of the country estate. This staging creates a greater challenge for an actor used to more traditional farces. Because the play takes place in two settings, and presents two plays simultaneously, the actor, even when not seen by the audience, must still say lines and perform actions backstage while remaining in character.

The central dramatic question of "Nothing On" is basically this: Will Lloyd Dallas be successful in creating a cohesive, entertaining production if it involves this eccentric band of divas, drunks, and oddballs? Dramaturgically, Lloyd, in the first two Act Ones, is set up to be the play's "straight man." Even though he refers to himself frequently as "God," he's not exactly the play's moral compass, as becomes clear fairly quickly, but he *is* the character that provides the standard by which normality and abnormality can be judged by the audience. Frayne sets the audience up to identify with Lloyd—even though Lloyd is no angel—in order for them to see this group of crazies and ne'er-do-wells through his eyes.

Farce and the Comic Actor

Remember, the characters in farce are often outsized, sometimes cartoonishly so. Therefore, analyzing your character for his major traits and characteristics, and then amplifying them, while still retaining the character's core humanity, is very important to the process of character building here.

Character Analysis

Farce may not demand a hundred-page backstory, but it does require a thorough analysis of the character's needs, obstacles, and tactics for each moment he is onstage—even when he is silent. The acting must always be truthful and grounded in the human reality of needs and wants.

So, identify and amplify your character's needs. If the need is great enough, it will not only provide a source of humor because of its incongruity, but will also ground the character in enough truth to sell the rest of the play's outlandishness. Find what your character desperately needs, what he can't live without, and then fight like hell to get it. Every character is in search of some treasure, be it success, love, control, or money and, in farce, this need must be amplified to the point of incongruity. Nothing is funnier than desperation.

Next, identify all the obstacles, even the most trivial, that are preventing your character from getting what he needs or wants. Always ask yourself, as the character: What is standing in your way? Identify all the obstacles, and then go after them with aggression and ingenuity. Always fight to win. That's what makes us want to watch your character.

Considering the personality, will, intellect, and emotional state of your character, what are the tactics or strategies they would use to surmount those obstacles? No idea is too outlandish, as long as it doesn't completely break with the circumstances of the play and the character.

Raise the stakes through the roof. They should be life or death, high enough to engender the urgency, and the desperation that needs to be there as the play accelerates toward the climax.

Energy and Tempo

Farce has special timing requirements. Each character has his own rhythm, and the trick is to bring all those different rhythms together to fit the tempo of the farce. This takes lots of rehearsals, exercises, and games to practice timing and working together smoothly as an ensemble.

As with most farces, time plays a huge factor. Time is running out. There's never enough time, and what little time there is, is subject to acceleration in farces. In this play, not having enough time proves to be a nightmare for the director, actors, and technicians. When things start to speed up, time gets away from the characters, and events start to unfold in a whirlwind of activity. This acceleration is matched by the passionate, near-explosive emotions gripping the backstage cast. By the third Act One, a sense of exhaustion settles on the entire cast, and time slows down again. The rhythm of "Nothing On" becomes incongruously slow, but that just adds to the humor of the farce within the farce. The "actors" no longer have any interest in playing their characters' needs and objectives with any energy, as they're too consumed by their own personal wants, battles, crises, and emotional highs and lows to worry about those of the character.

Conflict

Look for the infantile in your character. One of the central incongruities of the play is the reduction of the adult actors in the play to the behavior of children. It's funny because this group of theatre professionals has completely broken down into childish mayhem.

Find what frustrates your character and amplify it. Frustration and discomfort are the lifeblood of farce, which is, above all, about struggle. It's always about a fight—against time, against other people, against the self—so you, the actor, need to understand at every moment just what it is you're fighting for. The characters of farce on the stage suffer, hilariously, the improbable, often ridiculous circumstances of the plot.

Analyze the relationships and play them with what we call "amplified truth." If you love someone, you love them as if your life depended on it; if you need money, you need it as if your life depended on it, and so forth.

Status

Look for the status hierarchies and shifts. Farce is full of them. Over the course of the play, Lloyd is reduced from a somewhat arrogant, self-satisfied, theatre Lothario to a terrified, improvising stand-in for the Sheik. It's a radical loss of status and one of the funniest aspects of the character, and the play. It's his journey that the audience follows throughout, eager to see if he is successful or not. Overall, the play's status hierarchy can be evaluated as follows:

Dotty, as producer, she's the only one Lloyd treats with respect

Lloyd, the director

Garry, first Dotty's lover, then her arch-nemesis

Brooke, as Lloyd's lover, she rates fairly high on the status scale

Belinda, controls her world (and keeps her status high) by being the communicator, the gossip

Frederick, clueless and naïve, but with a good heart, which lowers his status

Selsdon, nearly washed up, and treated thusly

Poppy, stage manager with very little power over the cast. She is Lloyd's lover, though, which gives her a modicum of status

Tim, the lowest on the pole

By the end of the play, though, the statuses of the players on top of this hierarchy have shifted substantially, with Dotty and Lloyd defeated and near the bottom.

The Game

In Act Two (the second "Act One"), for example, the game is mainly that, as he's acting in "Nothing On," Garry constantly sees Dotty with Freddie and, misinterpreting what he sees, begins attacking the two of them. Dotty fights back and the rest of the cast is tasked with keeping them from killing each other, all the while trying to monitor Selsdon and his drinking.

Farce and *Noises Off*

For subject matter, farce tends to go after pretension, over-weaning pride, sanctimony, pomposity, and so forth. Lloyd's sin comes right out of the *lazzi* of *commedia dell'arte* or the Roman *phylax* plays: older man seeks sexual favors from young women. In that narrative tradition, his arrogance and self-satisfied demeanor ultimately give way to, by as early as the end of Act One, embarrassment and self-doubt.

Lloyd

Identify conflicts—All of the conflicts in the play, external, internal, those suffered by individual characters and the cast as a whole, are all essentially Lloyd's conflicts. The individuals in the cast *are* his obstacles, and their obstacles are his obstacles. His central objective is to put on a good production. That's what the audience sits there for two and a half hours for—to find out if he'll be successful. He is the one with the reputation to lose. And as all who work in the theatre know, you're only as good as your last show.

Identify major physical traits of the character—Generally fit, though aging. Reasonably attractive. Smoker.

Identify major psychological traits—Lloyd is generally guided by a somewhat arrogant, though generally benevolent, sense of self-assuredness. This façade can quickly fall away when things start to go wrong. He is insecure about his age, and pursues young women constantly to fill this vacuum. He has a love affair on every set, possibly as a result of a mid-life crisis. Gets nervous in stressful situations. Relies on pills to combat the stress.

Identify major emotional traits—He's generally calm, though somewhat arrogant and condescending, with a minor God complex. When things go wrong, he gets nervous episodes. His hands shake and he smokes and takes some type of prescription drug to relax him. But he has a mean streak, and a short temper that he lets fly on people he sees as weak.

The stakes for some characters are established as quite high by the faux biographies at the beginning of the play text. Some of these characters are at the end of their career and their popularity, like Dotty and Selsdon, so they want desperately for the production to be a success; Dotty in particular, because she is also a producer and has a financial stake in it:

Lloyd (*to* **Poppy**)   Ring the police.
Exit **Poppy** *into the wings*.
Lloyd (*to* **Tim**)   Finished the doors? Right, get the Burglar gear on.
[. . .]
Lloyd I'm sorry, Dotty, my love.
Dotty No, it's my fault, Lloyd, my love.

Lloyd I cast him.

Dotty "Let's give him one last chance," I said. "One last chance!" I mean, what can you do? We were in weekly rep together in Peebles.

Garry (*to* **Dotty**)   It's my fault, my precious. I shouldn't have let you. This tour for her isn't just, do you know what I mean? This is her life savings!

Lloyd We know that, Garry, love.

Belinda *puts a hand on* **Dotty**'s *arm.*

Dotty I'm not trying to make my fortune.

Frederick Of course you're not, Dotty.

Dotty I just wanted to put a little something by.

Belinda We know, love.[2]

(Act One [Act One])

As the end of the Act One rehearsal approaches, and the obstacles to a successful production seem to be mounting, Lloyd steadily loses his diplomatic sense of calm. When Freddie, at this very late hour, starts to question his character's motivation, it starts to infuriate Lloyd, who can barely contain his anger:

Lloyd Hold it. Freddie, what's the trouble?

Frederick Lloyd, you know how stupid I am about moves. Sorry, Garry … Sorry, Brooke … It's just my usual dimness. (*To* **Lloyd**.) But why do I take the things off into the study? Wouldn't it be more natural if I left them on?

Lloyd No.

Frederick I thought it might be somehow more logical.

Lloyd No.

Frederick Lloyd, I know it's a bit late in the day to go into all this …

Lloyd Freddie, we've got several more minutes left before we open.[3]

(Act One [Act One])

At first, he answers him flatly, "no," hoping this will deter Freddie from continuing his inquiry, but Freddie persists in his inopportune questioning, even getting Garry to begin questioning his character's actions. Freddie is, for Frayne, a symbol of that infuriating type of actor that needs to have every aspect of their character's motivation explained in detail, no matter if it holds up the rehearsal.

Lloyd then relents, stops the action, and lowers his status for all to see. He does something that is rare among directors: he admits that he doesn't know the answer. Freddie persists until Lloyd finally explodes in anger:

> **Frederick** All the same, if you could just give me a reason I could keep in my mind . . .
>
> **Lloyd** All right, I'll give you a reason. You carry those groceries into the study, Freddie, honey, because it's just slightly after midnight, and we're not going to be finished before we open tomorrow night. Correction—before we open *tonight*.
>
> **Frederick** *nods, rebuked, and exits into the study.* **Dotty** *silently follows him.* **Garry** *and* **Brooke** *go silently back into the bedroom.* **Lloyd** *returns to the stalls.*
>
> **Lloyd** And on we go. From after Freddie's exit, *with* the groceries.[4]

(Act One [Act One])

After this satisfying outburst, Lloyd is immediately shamed for it when Belinda drops a bomb:

> **Belinda** (*keeping her voice down*) Lloyd, sweetheart, his wife left him this morning.
>
> **Lloyd** Oh. (*Pause.*) Freddie!
>
> *Enter* **Frederick** *from the study*.
>
> **Lloyd** I think the point is that you've had a great fright when she mentions income tax, and you feel very insecure and exposed, and you want something familiar to hold on to.
>
> **Frederick** (*with humble gratitude*) Thank you, Lloyd. (*He clutches the groceries to his chest.*) That's most helpful.
>
> *Exit* **Frederick** *into the study.*[5]

(Act One [Act One])

Lloyd has to think quickly to repair Freddie's hurt feelings, changing his tone to one of sympathy and care and providing him with a workable motivation for his character.

Frayne creates a counterpoint to *Noises Off* by making "Nothing On" such an extreme farce. He demonstrates this by having almost all the actors constantly question the script, which is mired in improbabilities and contrived actions. This rough, unsophisticated script also becomes a huge obstacle for Lloyd. The actors are having difficulty because it doesn't make sense. And the more time that is lost trying to make sense of it, the more desperate and frustrated Lloyd becomes. This desperation comes to a hilarious head at the very end of the Act One rehearsal, when Brooke decides that she needs to discuss the logic of the script.

The problem with Lloyd's approach to the various obstacles that keep popping up regarding the script is that his emotional instability and attempts to solve the problems at hand just keep creating more problems. When Brooke says, "I don't understand why the Sheik looks like Philip,"[6] Lloyd has a meltdown and snaps, barking loudly at Brooke for refusing to say her line.

As she runs away, Lloyd realizes that he played the moment all wrong and rushes to console her. Belinda then reveals to the cast (and Poppy) that the two of them are having an affair. His self-praise is immediately cut short by Poppy saying, "I think I'm going to be sick"[7] and running away.

So, by the end of Act One, Lloyd is shamed by the revelations that he's carrying on a relationship with Brooke and Poppy, and a huge status shift has occurred. He thinks he's very clever, keeping it all a secret, and that no one knows his business, but the dramatic irony is that Belinda has just made the entire cast, and the audience, aware of his moral deficiencies.

Nothing is more terrifying to an actor than being unprepared for a production that is untried and untested. It's the stuff of nightmares. But, eventually, even that fear takes a backseat to the emotional beat-down happening backstage to the cast and crew. Just as in *commedia dell'arte*, everyone suffers some damage from the slapping stick.

No less, the hastily built set provides a number of physical obstacles to the characters: low-hanging ceilings, vertical beams, jutting wooden fixtures. As all seasoned actors know, backstage can be a perilous place, so clearly it provides the perfect environment for a farce, where the space can and should actively contribute to the danger and desperation confronting the characters. The fact that the tempo of the action rises and rises until it hits a fever pitch just increases the sense of danger the audience experiences. Farce requires hours and hours of rehearsal to get every movement, intonation, and gesture right, and to prevent any "real" harm to the actor.

Often having an absurdly limited time frame within which to work as well as handling multiple projects, directors offer incredible comic potential in that their stakes are always high, and the more successful they are, the more money gets invested. And since farce loves pain, a director is a perfect source of humor. A director's job/life is about constantly putting out fires, unendingly confronting obstacles, and using tactics to overcome them or creating solutions that help others to overcome *their* obstacles:

> **Lloyd** Tim, let me tell you something about *my* life. I have the Duke of Buckingham on the phone to me an hour after rehearsal every evening complaining that the Duke of Gloucester is sucking boiled sweets through his speeches. The Duke of Clarence is off for the entire week doing a commercial for Madeira. Richard himself—would you believe?—Richard III? (*He demonstrates.*)—has now gone down with a back problem. I keep getting messages from Brooke about how unhappy she is here and now she's got herself a doctor's certificate for nervous exhaustion—she's going to walk! I have no time to find and rehearse another Vicki. I have just one afternoon, while Richard is fitted for a surgical corset, to cure Brooke of nervous exhaustion, with no medical aids except a little bit of whisky— you've got the whisky?—a few flowers—you've got the money for the flowers?—and a certain faded charm. [. . .][8]

(Act Two [Act One])

Lloyd is swamped with obstacles: two shows, both of them disasters, two relationships in peril, and a very short amount of time to solve what he thinks is the most pressing problem, Brooke. He is soon to realize, however, that he has far greater problems with this show. His first clue that something is terribly wrong with it is in the "front of house" calls to the audience, explaining how many minutes until the curtain opens. Poppy and Tim become confused in the melee backstage as to who is supposed to give the calls, and they repeat each other, confusing the audience and contributing to Lloyd's vicious outburst backstage:

Lloyd What the fuck is going on?
Belinda Lloyd!
Frederick Great Scott!
Poppy I didn't know you were here!
Lloyd I'm *not* here. I'm at the Aberystwyth Festival! But I can't sit out there and listen to "two minutes … three minutes … one minute … two minutes!"
Belinda My sweet, we're having great dramas downstairs!
Lloyd We're having great dramas out there! (*To* **Poppy**.) This is the matinée, honey! There's old-age pensioners out there! "The curtain will rise in three minutes"—we all start for the Gents. "The curtain will rise in one minute"—we all come running out again. We don't know which way we're going![9]

(Act Two [Act One])

Lloyd explodes through the stage door in a fit of rage, just as Poppy gives the final errant house call, amplifying the surprise and humor. Even this early in the play, Lloyd is slightly unhinged. His strategy of coming in quietly and slipping up to Brooke's room unnoticed is a failure. His need to fix the show, to make it good, has to be so jacked up that he can't sit by in the audience and listen to what's happening. He gives up his plan and goes backstage to sort the situation out.

By the third Act One, the audience is the last thing on the players' minds, and this incongruity becomes the premise for the nonstop hilarity of the third act; what we expect the actors to care about—putting on a good show for us—they could care less about, being so caught up in the back-biting, aggression, and violence happening backstage. It's their complete absorption in what's happening interpersonally between them, instead of what's happening onstage, that makes this section of the play so funny.

By now, the performance has completely broken down into vendettas and interpersonal warfare, which raises the stakes for Lloyd even more. The lines from "Nothing On" have now become interspersed with the personal information of the actors and the show is in danger of completely falling apart. Lloyd fights until the end to save the show, though, never giving up. When he thinks that Selsdon is not going on as the burglar, he assumes the role, breaking into the house and discovering that they are already both on as the burglar. The only thing they can all do is say their lines and do their actions. Finally, Flavia has an idea about how to break the burglar monotony, and she puts the responsibility for saving them all on Lloyd's shoulders:

> **Burglar/Lloyd** No bars. No burglar alarms. They ought to be prosecuted for incitement.
> *He climbs in, very uncertain what's happening to him. He doesn't know whether to react to the presence of the others or not.*
> **Mrs. Clackett** They always come in threes, don't they.
> **All Three Burglars** When I think I used to do banks! When I remember I used to do bullion vaults . . .
> **Flavia** Hold on! We know this man! He's not a burglar.
> *She snatches **Lloyd**'s **Burglar** hat off.*
> He's our social worker!
> **Roger** He's *what*?
> **Flavia** He's that nice man who comes in and tells us all *what to do*!
> **Lloyd** (*appalled, faintly*) What to do?
> **Others** (*firmly*) What to do![10]

(Act Three [Act One])

Lloyd is empty, he has nothing left in his tank, and all he can do is mutter excuses. His last suggestion for how to get out of their quandary only causes more problems:

> **Selsdon** What's he saying?
> **Flavia** He's saying, he's saying—just get through it for doors and sardines! Yes? That's what it's all about! Doors and sardines! (*To **Lloyd**.*) Yes?
> **Lloyd** (*helplessly*) Doors and sardines!
> **Others** Doors and sardines!
> *They all try to put this into practice. **Philip** picks up the sardines and runs around trying to find some application for them. The others open various doors, fetch further plates of sardines, and run helplessly around with them. **Lloyd** stands helplessly watching the chaos he has created swirl around him.*

Flavia He's saying, he's saying—"Phones and police!"

Lloyd Phones and police . . .

Philip Phone!

Philip *and* **Roger** *are each handed a half of the phone.*

Roger Police!

Roger *puts the receiver to his ear.* **Philip** *dials.*

Flavia He's saying "Bags and boxes."

Others Bags and boxes!

Everyone runs around with the two boxes and the two bags, all
*   helplessly colliding with each other and running into the furniture.*

Flavia (*decisively*)　Sheets, sheets! He's saying "Sheets!"

Lloyd Sheets . . .

Others (*desperately*)　Sheets![11]

(Act Three [Act One])

Lloyd is now at the end of his rope. The leader of the production, the person who started out the play with the highest status, the man with all the answers, is now totally helpless without the help of the other cast members. This status shift is hilarious and not tragic because Lloyd kind of deserves what he gets because of the way he treats others. At the beginning of the play, he arrogantly compares his job as director to that of God. But at the end, broken, defeated, all he can do is try to run away and lick his wounds.

Comedy developed out of rustic, folk comedies, but somewhere along the way, it lost the wildness and unpredictability and grounded itself in the rules of logic and probability. Comedy demands a level of truth in its events, situations, and characters that farce does not. Because it is grounded in reality, characters are generally expected to be fully fleshed out, internally and externally. Comedy aims for a sense of probability, whereas farce can fully embrace the ridiculous and the completely improbable. Those incongruities are doubled in *Noises Off*, with two different plays going on simultaneously. With farce, it is crucially important for the actor to take these to a level even higher than expected. This keeps the audience on its toes, keeps the tension high, and gives the actor a wonderful range for physical actions.

* * *

We like to kid our students by saying, "Shakespeare's isn't so special—he's just another playwright." When they protest, we agree sheepishly, "Oh, sure, he's very good—very, *very* good—but ..." That "but" allows us to get to the central point. He is still a playwright, even if he is *the* playwright among playwrights, and so, in his comedies, the same theories about why we laugh, the same rules for the actor, the same "elements" of the comic character, the same psychological and performance issues, the same evolution of the comic character from the beginning to the end of the play—in effect, the topics of the previous chapters—apply, and the comic actor, given the chance to do Shakespeare, can apply them all.

Accordingly, in the next chapter, we focus on the "options" that this rich playwright offers his actors; the choices the actor can make, the way his particular take on a character will influence his delivery and movement, the subtext he brings to the character, his relation both as an actor and as a character to his fellow actors. Shakespeare is not prescriptive: an actor himself, he surely knew that actors like to have a hand in creating the character.

In Chapter 7, we suggest various options for the actors in five of Shakespeare's best-known comedies: *The Comedy of Errors*, *The Taming of the Shrew*, *Twelfth Night*, *Much Ado about Nothing*, and that wretched funny production of *Pyramus and Thisbe* in *A Midsummer Night's Dream*.

An afterthought: might the subtitle of *Twelfth Night—What You Will—* have something to do with this idea of options?

Notes

1 Michael Frayn, *Noises Off* (London: Bloomsbury Methuen Drama, 2011).
2 Frayn, *Noises Off*, 24–5.
3 Ibid., 33–4.
4 Ibid., 36.
5 Ibid., 36–7.
6 Ibid., 68.
7 Ibid., 70.
8 Ibid., 76.
9 Ibid., 82.
10 Ibid., 162.
11 Ibid., 162–3.

7

OPTIONS IN PLAYING SHAKESPEARE'S COMEDY

Theatre historians disagree as to just how stylized comedic acting was in Shakespeare's day.[1] To what degree was the acting presentational? Or was it often more natural, especially with low-life characters? Did the actor playing Sir Toby Belch in *Twelfth Night* make him more real and therefore immediate to the Globe audience of average citizens than, say, the Duchess Olivia, who, after all, is something of a poseur wearing a black veil during a yearlong period of mourning for her brother? Then there is Shakespeare's language—rich, laden with metaphor, playful, reflective of his large treasure chest of words and phrases: To what degree does this affect the acting, especially when we stage a Shakespearean comedy today? Such questions must be kept in mind as we look at the range of challenges presented to the actor and director. We can, of course, explore the world of Shakespeare's comedy by tracing the history of acting styles and conventions from the Renaissance onward. Equally, though, the director and actor will want to use what works with a modern audience, respectful of the past, indebted to it, but also conversant with the acting styles and conventions of our own theatre.

Shakespeare's humor ranges from the bawdy to the political; from one-liners, innuendos, and set-up comic routines to those profound moments in which comedy is the operating principle, the means by which playwright and actor make the character rich, complex, and human. Nor are his comedies so easily separated from his tragedies or serious drama. At the end of *A Midsummer Night's Dream*, as the audience in the house watch Oberon, Titania, and Puck watch Theseus, and his court watch Bottom and his company stage their wretched but also wonderfully funny *Pyramus and Thisbe*, each audience thinks it is real, live men and women watching a show. But in his epilogue, Puck challenges us: Have we only dreamed we were here? Are we only figures in a larger play, a "dream," watching the palpable illusion of the stage? In *King Lear*, Shakespeare mixes comedy and tragedy—the Fool's bawdy, spot-on humor, his cruel jokes, playing counterpoint to the old man's suffering on the heath. That mixture gets more complicated if, as has been done in productions over the years, we double the parts of the Fool and Cordelia. In their way, Shakespeare's comedies are as profound, as "rich and strange" (*The Tempest*, 1.2.565),[2] as his tragedies.

Even when his humor is limited to the predictable or conventional, such as an insult line or a stock situation, Shakespeare's jokes, even the most obvious, grossest ones, are woven into the play's larger patterns, and contribute to what is happening onstage—visually, psychologically, even politically. Playing them demands from the actor real ability, thought, dedication—and practice. The actor needs to think about what the joke is doing for both his delivery and character, how it is contributing to the situation at hand, and how it fits in with the larger pattern of the play.

The Comic Routine: *The Comedy of Errors*

In workshops, we often use the following scene between Antipholus and Dromio of Syracuse ("Antipholus S." and "Dromio S.," respectively, below) in *The Comedy of Errors* because it is as funny as Shakespeare can be, using crude, body-based humor juxtaposed with puns and wit. On the surface, it may even look like little more than the comic sketch you'd see at some club. Only on the surface, that is, though:

Antipholus S. How dost thou mean, a fat marriage?
Dromio S. Marry, sir, she's the kitchen wench, and all grease
[. . .].

Antipholus S. What's her name?

Dromio S. Nell, sir; but her name and three quarters, that's an ell and three quarters, will not measure her from hip to hip [. . .]; she is spherical, like a globe; I could find out countries in her.

Antipholus S. In what part of her body stands Ireland?

Dromio S. Marry, sir, in her buttocks; I found it out by the bogs.

Antipholus S. Where Scotland?

Dromio S. I found it by the barrenness, hard in the palm of the hand.

Antipholus S. Where France?

Dromio S. In her forehead, armed and reverted, making war against her heir.

Antipholus S. Where England?

Dromio S. I looked for the chalky cliffs, but I could find no whiteness in them. But I guess it stood in her chin, by the salt rheum that ran between France and it.

Antipholus S. Where Spain.

Dromio S. Faith, I saw it not; but I felt it hot in her breath.

Antipholus S. Where America, the Indies?

Dromio S. O, sir, upon her nose, all o'er-embellished with rubies, carbuncles, sapphires, declining their rich aspect to the hot breath of Spain, who sent whole armadoes of carracks to be ballast at her nose.

Antipholus S. Where stood Belgia, the Netherlands?

Dromio S. O, sir, I did not look so low. To conclude, this drudge or diviner laid claim to me, called me Dromio, swore I was assured to her, told me what privy marks I had about me, as the mark of my shoulder, the mole in my neck, the great wart on my [*beat*] left arm, that I, amazed, ran from her as a witch.[3]

(3.2.94–143 [*with some cuts made*])

Given the near impossibility of a comic set-up in which two pairs of twins are in the same town on the same day, with neither twin knowing his brother is present, it was inevitable something like this would happen: a very large kitchen wench who is engaged to Dromio of Ephesus confuses Dromio of Syracuse for her betrothed.[4]

Dromio of Syracuse comes rushing up to his master with this shocking news. Maybe he even likes the idea of being loved, though he might have preferred someone thinner. If he clutches his heart with one hand and shakes the other as if in terror, he sends mixed signals to Antipholus of Syracuse. The word "fat" throws his master: Does it mean overweight or "potentially prosperous"? When Dromio denigrates the very woman whose ardor intrigues him—she's only a fat kitchen wench and greasy at that—we get one of those sudden emotional changes endemic to comedy. This comic moment allows the master and servant to abandon for a time what they thought was their past identity.

First, Antipholus sets up Dromio for a series of bawdy puns and double entendres, comedy seemingly without any larger purpose than getting a laugh from the audience. However, the actors can ground that laughter in the fact that the master takes a growing pleasure in being the straight man to the servant, while underneath both are simultaneously terrified and intrigued, trying to find their footing in an illusory and threatening world.

The immediate threat is known as Nell, whose name admits a bad pun, but an appropriate one, since the woman is very wide and threatening, an "ell [i.e., a measurement of more than a yard] and three quarters." Perhaps here Dromio can play a merchant giving a prospective buyer a product's weight or measurement. Delighted that his pun gets a small, appreciative laugh from his master, he ups the stakes with a simile: she is "spherical like the globe." The words practically beg for physical action. Taking the bait, Antipholus steps back, his hands outstretched as if asking, "Can she be this big around?" Pushing his master's hands even farther apart, Dromio then gets a sympathetic nod from Antipholus: she is even wider than he imagines! The simile is more literal than poetic.

Then, sympathy extended, but knowing that servants like to be witty—after all, this is what endears Dromio to Antipholus—the master, like a schoolteacher, initiates today's geography test. What if Dromio dances about the stage as he calls out the countries of Europe, each getting its own physical shtick from the comic: a slap of the master's backside for Ireland, rubbing his palm like some stingy Scotsman fondling coins, converting his nose into the chalky cliffs of England, and then running his fingers down to the chin, the runny nose becoming "salt rheum," exhaling inches in front of his face as Antipholus staggers back at the "hot breath" of Spain. Intimate with the master's body as no respectable servant ever would be, in Shakespeare's day or our own, the straight man steps back for emphasis—he has one more country in mind: the Netherlands. Faking embarrassment, "O, sir, I did not look so low," Dromio can play a caricature of the servant deeply offended that his master could even ask such a rude question. Then, he delivers his conclusion: the final proof that this strange woman somehow knows him being her intimate knowledge of his "privy marks," such as that on his shoulder and the mole on his neck.

The routine over, the diversion has served its purpose of momentarily allowing master and servant to forget the "amazement" (in the double sense of wonder and terror) of being in Ephesus, described in *Saint Paul* as a town of magicians and sorcerers.[5] These two men of such unequal stature come to delight in each other's company, enjoying sharing puns and jokes. The comic routine signals their closeness as they each search for a lost twin brother.

Comedy as a Verbal and Physical Battle: *The Taming of the Shrew*

Petruchio Come, come, you wasp; i'faith, you are too angry.

Katherina If I be waspish, best beware my sting.

Petruchio My remedy is, then, to pluck it out.

Katherina Ay, if the fool could find it where it lies.

Petruchio Who knows not where a wasp does wear his sting? In his tail.

Katherina In his tongue.

Petruchio Whose tongue?

Katherina Yours, if you talk of tales; and so farewell.

Petruchio What, with my tongue in your tail? Nay, come again. Good Kate, I am a gentleman—[6]

(2.1.209–19)

Beyond their conscious knowledge at this point, Petruchio, an arrogant, money-seeking misogynist, and Katherina, a man-hating shrew, may be attracted to each other. If you play Petruchio, you get to deliver one of the bawdiest lines in Shakespeare: as you leer at the actress playing Kate, adopting the tactic of "you said it, not me," you charge her with suggesting that you lick her backside, putting your "tongue in [her] tail." If the joke were nothing more than this, Shakespeare would be no better than the nightclub comedian trying to get a cheap laugh. Here, though, the actor needs to avoid just playing the joke. Oh, he'll get a laugh out of "tongue in your tail," but he has to make this remark grow out of his character, the truth of who Petruchio really is, the man Kate will celebrate in her final speech at the wedding banquet.

One way of playing the situation, which culminates in that otherwise gross line, is to take it as the mutual product of the two actors, this seemingly contentious couple. That is, Kate purposely sets up Petruchio and he in turn sets up her. She feeds him material for the joke; after all, she's the one who specifies it is to be *his* tongue, though he interrupts her with "Whose tongue?" just to make sure he's hearing her right. Kate can move away from him, this time confident as she pins him with the "tongue" and then puns on "tale/tail." She's won. The scene is over. He's good, better than all the rest, but not quite her equal, and Kate wants someone who is at least that, if not superior. Still, once again, she's wrong, for he raises that bawdy question, "My tongue in your tail?" He'll forgive her; she can "come again" and rejoin their duet. At each other's throats, at least verbally, nevertheless, the two actors as well as the two characters, despite their playing at being hostile, are connecting.

The point is that the joke becomes a mutual product, and thus part of the larger pattern in which, despite their surface violence, their verbal battles—one production we saw had them spar in a boxing ring[7]— Kate and Petruchio really enjoy each other's company, having waited a lifetime for each other. Might their apparent dislike ultimately be a defensive screen? In truth, they long for each other, and are thrilled that they have finally found someone worthy of their love, not to mention their verbal skills. His interest in her is not just money or sex, but the bond of friendship and mutual respect between a gentleman and a gentlewoman—for that's what Kate is down deep, beneath her surface image. That is how he sees her.

In reality, Kate doesn't need to be tamed by Petruchio, and Petruchio's professed misogyny extends to everyone *but* Kate. They were meant for each other. And they *like* to play, to joke, to pretend.

Like Beatrice and Benedick in *Much Ado about Nothing*, they are giants of wit and energy and passion, purposely overreacting in a world of dullards, conventional characters, and genuine shrews, like Bianca.

What would happen if you gave half of Kate's final big speech about wifely "obedience" to Petruchio, sending the signal to the audience that the speech could just as easily have been delivered by the man as the woman?[8] Together, they are talking not about inequality or subservience, let alone sexual domination, but a love where one sacrifices himself or herself for the other, where in mutual service they establish true equality. In this first meeting of the two antagonists, then, the actors must strike a balance between the physicality of their battle and the meaning underneath the surface wit if the comedy is to become transparent.

Conscious and Unconscious Comics: *Twelfth Night*

Kinsman to the haughty Duchess Olivia, his very name announcing the nature of this stock comic character, Sir Toby Belch is what we might today call a functioning alcoholic. Lusty, given to sowing confusion, disorder, and practical jokes, this Falstaff transformed into the world of *Twelfth Night* takes a special pleasure in bringing down straight-laced Puritans like Malvolio, and, no less, taking advantage of shallow courtiers, "ninnies" as they are called in Shakespeare, like Sir Andrew Aguecheek. His partner in crime is Maria, Olivia's lady-in-waiting, who's not a menial but a confidant, the witty servant so common in Shakespeare. Watch what happens when Sir Toby and Maria play with the foppish and utterly gullible Sir Andrew:

Sir Andrew Sir Toby Belch! How now, Sir Toby Belch?

Sir Toby Sweet Sir Andrew!

Sir Andrew Bless you, fair shrew.

Maria And you too, sir.

Sir Toby Accost, Sir Andrew, accost.

Sir Andrew What's that?

Sir Toby My niece's chambermaid.

Sir Andrew Good Mistress Accost, I desire better acquaintance.

Maria My name is Mary, sir.

Sir Andrew Good Mistress Mary Accost—

Sir Toby You mistake, knight. "Accost" is front her, board her, woo
her, assail her.

Sir Andrew By my troth, I would not undertake her in this company.
Is that the meaning of "accost"?

Maria Fare you well, gentlemen.

Sir Toby And thou let part so, Sir Andrew, would thou might'st
never draw sword again!

Sir Andrew And you part so, mistress, I would I might never draw
sword again. Fair lady, do you think you have fools in hand?

Maria Sir, I have not you by th' hand.

Sir Andrew Marry, but you shall have, and here's my hand.

Maria Now, sir, thought is free. I pray you bring your hand to th'
buttery bar and let it drink.

Sir Andrew Wherefore, sweetheart? What's your metaphor?

Maria It's dry, sir.

Sir Andrew Why, I think so: I am not such an ass but I can keep my
hand dry. But what's your jest?

Maria A dry jest, sir.

Sir Andrew Are you full of them?

Maria Ay, sir, I have them at my fingers' ends: marry, now I let go
your hand, I am barren. (*Exit* **Maria**.)[9]

(1.3.44–78)

The three actors constitute a trio whose key signature is the word
"accost."[10] Sir Andrew has boasted of being proficient in many
languages, fancies himself a sophisticated courtier. This parody of a
knight falls head over heels in love with Maria, possibly rushing over
to her a split second after he has taken the stage, thrusting his face
indiscreetly close to hers, not even acknowledging Sir Toby's greeting.
Sir Toby has to instruct him to stop staring at the woman and attend
to social niceties such as "accosting" or greeting her. Since Sir Toby
himself fancies her, his instruction can be delivered harshly, designed to
put down a potential rival.

The actor playing Sir Toby has two options: Is he just trying to get
his friend to say hello, or, since he knows Sir Andrew all too well, is he
aiding this fool in putting his foot further and further in his mouth? How
deliberate, for example, is the sexual pun on the alternative meanings

he now offers for "accost"—"front her, board her, woo her, assail her"? He can deliver the bawdy meaning of "accost" with a straight face to his rival, winking at his mistress with a subtext of "this ninny's so aroused by you that I bet, despite all his pretenses of being a sophisticated courtier, he won't be able to hold back his lust any better than some rude villager." Sir Toby proves right. Sir Andrew's sexual desire for Maria comes rushing to the surface: he proffers the qualification that he would not "accost" her, in the way he thinks Sir Toby is suggesting, "in this [present] company."

Much to Sir Toby's surprise, Maria has had enough of the straight man and his unwitting stooge, and, brushing by both men, heads for the exit. Thinking quickly, Sir Toby goes on a witty offensive, taunting Sir Andrew: if he lets this woman depart in this mood, he will probably never be able to "draw [his] sword again." Sir Andrew takes the bait if not the innuendo in "sword"; he finds no sexual double meaning in his "Fair lady, do you think you have fools in hand?"

Maria now takes charge, asserts her rights as a liberated woman, and rejects his advances by assuring him that she, repulsed by his clumsy foreplay, will never have him "by the hand." Sir Andrew just doesn't get it: he extends his literal hand. Again she refuses it, playing on the fact that, like his hand, both he and his attempt at wit are dry or barren. She is verbally playful, suggestive; the witless Sir Andrew is horribly literal. With her exit line, she plays once more on "barren"—she is now out of wit, barren, can't go any further with such a fool.

What we have called the "range" of Shakespeare's comedy is never so evident as when, later in the play, he gives the actor playing Sir Andrew a single line that adds depth to this otherwise stock character:

Sir Toby Good night, Penthesilea.
Sir Andrew Before me, she's a good wench.
Sir Toby She's a beagle, true-bred, and one that adores
    me: what o' that?
Sir Andrew I was adored once too.[11]

(2.3.174–8)

The actor playing Sir Andrew has had almost two full scenes to set his character. Andrew is so absurd he's lovable. But there is, so far, no depth to him. Now, as he watches Maria exit and Sir Toby, her lover, bid her a comic but also tender "Good night" with his pseudo-Greek "Penthesilea" (the queen of the Amazons and hence a loving joke about Maria's size), Sir Andrew, consumed with envy, wishes he could exchange places with his friend.

Sir Toby, oblivious to Sir Andrew's presence, stares longingly at the spot where Maria has made her exit. Trying to call his friend back to the present, Sir Andrew says something that he thinks might please his friend: he calls Maria "a good wench." Sir Toby at first downplays Maria's charms, comparing her, instead, to a well-bred dog, but then he says the one thing that rekindles Andrew's envy: she is "one that adores" him. Even this he dismisses with "What o' that?" He has her, he can joke about her, and even mildly insult the woman. This is what you can do if you're confident in your abilities as a lover. But, to know such confidence, you have to have someone who loves you in return.

Then comes the line we're after: Sir Andrew Aguecheek's plaintive (surely that is one way of delivering it) "I was adored once too." What would happen if he crossed downstage and delivered the line straight to the audience, breaking the fourth wall? There are lots of options for the actor here. Perhaps he is lying, trying to make himself Sir Toby's equal by summoning up a fictive lover. Or the line may come from deep within him, a subtext for a character we have, up to now, written off as shallow.

Whatever option you take in *Twelfth Night*, the actor here has the chance to show a new dimension of Aguecheek: beneath the fool is a man who was once loved, once valued. He has not always been the fool. The otherwise stock comic character is not just that. His bittersweet line enhances the role of the comic actor.

The Comedy of Romance: *Much Ado about Nothing*

Having broken off their engagement months before the play begins, Beatrice and Benedick now spend their time bickering, like Kate and Petruchio. A source of amusement for their audience, whether large or small, that bickering has, so far, been in public. But no one is around when they meet in the famous "Kill Claudio" scene.

Benedick comes upon Beatrice weeping for the humiliation of her best friend Hero. His objective is clear: she's weeping, she's vulnerable, and this is his chance to resume his courtship. However, he makes his move at the wrong time. In no mood for love, Beatrice wants someone to revenge Hero:

Benedick Lady Beatrice, have you wept all this while?

Beatrice Yea, and I will weep a while longer.

Benedick I will not desire that.

Beatrice You have no reason, I do it freely.

Benedick Surely I do believe your fair cousin is wronged.

Beatrice Ah, how much might the man deserve of me that would right her!

Benedick Is there any way to show such friendship?

Beatrice A very even way, but no such friend.

Benedick May a man do it?

Beatrice It is a man's office, but not yours.[12]

(4.1.254–65)

Talk about the comic character's self-ignorance—a comically ardent man unaware that he is only turning off the woman. Single-minded in his objective, he thinks he's being gallant: first setting a limit for weeping (a possible subtext: "Surely you can't have been weeping this long—it's unnatural"), then setting himself up as the arbiter of weeping ("I will not desire that"), and, after these two mistakes, telling her what she already knows, that Hero has been "wronged." "What an ass," Beatrice must be thinking, "This is the worst pick-up I've ever heard!"

But there's an interesting option for the actor playing Beatrice: What if her weeping is only fake? That is, as Benedick approaches her, she only pretends to weep. She has an ulterior motive for such acting: she needs him not as a lover but as an avenger, and so draws this lovesick fool into her trap, even insulting his manhood by dismissing him as unqualified for the "office."

Next, there's one of those quick changes of emotions we've identified with comic characters. Now aware that he's doing everything wrong, Benedick throws away what he thought was a subtle approach to the woman and blurts out what's really on his mind. Whatever both actors have established so far is thrown to the wind:

Benedick I do love nothing in the world so well as you—is not that strange?

Beatrice As strange as the thing I know not. It were as possible for me to say I loved nothing so well as you, but believe me not; and yet I lie not; I confess nothing, nor I deny nothing. I am sorry for my cousin.

Benedick By my sword, Beatrice, thou lovest me.[13]

(4.1.266–72)

Poor Hero is rudely forgotten. However confident an actor Beatrice might have been at the top of the scene, now she's losing it. Benedick makes a simple "manly" declaration of love, while Beatrice, every bit his equal in the play, here falls into the chauvinist's characterization of a woman who cannot make up her mind: she loves Benedick in turn, yet she doesn't love him; don't believe her when she says she does, but don't think she's lying. Drowning, she fights to get back on topic: "I am sorry for my cousin." Benedick pulls her back to the real issue of the scene: love, not Hero.

A matter of status change—she was up and now she's down. Just the reverse for Benedick. So, now they're equal. Having failed to keep up those personas that worked so successfully when they had an audience, now, in their ardor, their excitement, even their fear of falling in love again, they unconsciously parody the very image of Renaissance lovers. Shakespeare—maliciously?—gives the actors here some of the worst poetry he's ever written:

Benedick By my sword, Beatrice, thou lovest me.

Beatrice Do not swear and eat it.

Benedick I will swear by it that you love me, and I will make him eat it that says I love not you.

Beatrice Will you not eat your word?

Benedick With no sauce that can be devised to it. I protest I love thee.[14]

(4.1.272–7)

Beatrice's objective is to make sure Benedick is being truthful; his, to convince her he is just that. The more the actors make us believe their characters feel they are being clever with this mangled metaphor—false vows are like bad sauce spread on a sword and anyone denying the lover's vow would have to eat it!—the funnier the exchange is. They are a far cry from the witty couple who entertained the court in the opening scene. A simple, metaphor-free line mercifully stops all this: "I love thee."

So, three comic shifts so far: Benedick unwittingly playing the fool, and perhaps tricked into doing so by Beatrice; then it's her turn to take on that role; and finally, the silly sauce metaphor, with both characters unaware of just how their bad poetry might be received by others—we in the house can play the court here.

And what of the moment we've been waiting for: Beatrice's simple "Kill Claudio." Is this a suggestion, a command, or a desperate attempt to make sure Benedick doesn't abandon her? There are lots of options here for the actor.

> **Beatrice** Why, then, God forgive me!
> **Benedick** What offence, sweet Beatrice?
> **Beatrice** You have stayed me in a happy hour, I was about to protest I loved you.
> **Benedick** And do it with all thy heart.
> **Beatrice** I love you with so much of my heart that none is left to protest.
> **Benedick** Come, bid me do anything for thee.
> **Beatrice** Kill Claudio![15]

> (4.1.279–87)

Given the "performance" of these two so far in the scene, as they try to find some solid ground on which to stand and, in the process, turn into lovers not much different from Claudio and Hero whom they both mocked earlier in the play, how seriously can the audience take Beatrice's "Kill Claudio"? For that matter, how seriously does she take it? Sure, she wants to make sure Benedick's vow of love is sincere, will last, but why such an extreme test? How the actor delivers the climactic line will determine the audience's response. Would your take on the situation here lead to "understanding" laughter that these two characters, who otherwise think themselves superior to everyone else in the play, have got themselves in this pickle? In the nineteenth century, *Much Ado* was often billed as *Beatrice and Benedick*. The one saving grace here is that at least they are now refocused on Hero's condition.

The Theatre Itself as Comedy: *A Midsummer Night's Dream*

Within *A Midsummer Night's Dream*,[16] the wretchedly amateur production *Pyramus and Thisbe* nonetheless reminds the audience, though not the aristocrats onstage, of what would have been Hermia's fate if there had been no forest to which she and Lysander could escape, no supernatural beings waiting there to convert a potential tragedy to a comedy. Bottom's production also evokes that other play of star-crossed lovers Shakespeare wrote in 1595, *Romeo and Juliet*. Even as Bottom blurs the distinction between the stage and reality, Duke Theseus clings to what he takes as his sure, ordered world of Athens, and has no sympathy for the fantastic story the four lovers tell of their night in the forest.[17]

Here's the scene:

Pyramus O grim-look'd night! O night with hue so black!
O night, which ever art when day is not!
O night, O night! alack, alack, alack,
I fear my Thisbe's promise is forgot!
And thou, O wall, O sweet, O lovely wall,
That stand'st between her father's ground and mine!
Thou wall, O wall, O sweet and lovely wall,
Show me thy chink, to blink through with mine eyne!
Wall *holds up his fingers.*
Thanks, courteous wall: Jove shield thee well for this!
But what see I? No Thisbe do I see.
O wicked wall, through whom I see no bliss!
Cursed be thy stones for thus deceiving me!
Theseus The wall, methinks, being sensible, should curse again.
Pyramus No, in truth, sir, he should not. "Deceiving me" is Thisbe's
cue: she is to enter now, and I am to spy her through the wall.
You shall see it will fall pat as I told you: yonder she comes.
Enter **Thisbe***.*
Thisbe O wall, full often hast thou heard my moans,
For parting my fair Pyramus and me!
My cherry lips have often kiss'd thy stones,
Thy stones with lime and hair knit up in thee.

Pyramus I see a voice; now will I to the chink,
To spy an I can hear my Thisbe's face.
Thisbe?
Thisbe. My love thou art, my love I think!
Pyramus Think what thou wilt, I am thy lover's grace;
And like Limander am I trusty still.
Thisbe And I like Helen, till the Fates me kill.
Pyramus Not Shafalus to Procrus was so true.
Thisbe As Shafalus to Procrus, I to you.
Pyramus O kiss me through the hole of this vile wall.
Thisbe I kiss the wall's hole, not your lips at all.
Pyramus Wilt thou at Ninny's tomb meet me straightway?
Thisbe 'Tide life, 'tide death, I come without delay.
Exeunt **Pyramus** *and* **Thisbe**.

. . .

Enter **Lion** *and* **Moonshine**.
Lion You ladies, you whose gentle hearts do fear
The smallest monstrous mouse that creeps on floor,
May now, perchance, both quake and tremble here,
When lion rough in wildest rage doth roar.
Then know that I as Snug the joiner am
A lion-fell, nor else no lion's dam;
For if I should as lion come in strife
Into this place, 'twere pity on my life.

. . .

Enter **Thisbe**.
Thisbe This is old Ninny's tomb. Where is my love?
Lion (*roaring*)   Oh—
Thisbe *runs off.*

. . .

Enter **Pyramus**.
Pyramus Sweet Moon, I thank thee for thy sunny beams;
I thank thee, Moon, for shining now so bright;
For by thy gracious, golden, glittering gleams,
I trust to take of truest Thisbe sight.
But stay! O spite!
But mark, poor knight,
What dreadful dole is here?

Eyes, do you see?
How can it be?
O dainty duck! O dear!
Thy mantle good,
What! Stain'd with blood?
Approach, ye Furies fell!
O Fates, come, come!
Cut thread and thrum;
Quail, crush, conclude, and quell.

Theseus This passion, and the death of a dear friend, would go
near to make a man look sad.

Hippolyta Beshrew my heart, but I pity the man.

Pyramus O wherefore, Nature, didst thou lions frame?
Since lion vile hath here deflower'd my dear:
Which is—no, no—which was the fairest dame
That lived, that loved, that liked, that look'd with cheer.
Come, tears, confound;
Out, sword, and wound
The pap of Pyramus;
Ay, that left pap,
Where heart doth hop:
Stabs himself.
Thus die I, thus, thus, thus.
Now am I dead,
Now am I fled;
My soul is in the sky:
Tongue, lose thy light;
Moon, take thy flight:
Exit **Moonshine**.
Now die, die, die, die, die.
Dies.

. . .

Re-enter **Thisbe**.

Thisbe Asleep, my love?
What, dead, my dove?
O Pyramus, arise!
Speak, speak. Quite dumb?
Dead, dead? A tomb

Must cover thy sweet eyes.
These My lips,
This cherry nose,
These yellow cowslip cheeks,
Are gone, are gone:
Lovers, make moan:
His eyes were green as leeks.
O Sisters Three,
Come, come to me,
With hands as pale as milk;
Lay them in gore,
Since you have shore
With shears his thread of silk.
Tongue, not a word:
Come, trusty sword;
Come, blade, my breast imbrue:
Stabs herself.
And, farewell, friends;
Thus Thisbe ends:
Adieu, adieu, adieu.
Dies. [18]

(5.1.169–334)

Like the aristocratic audience, we laugh in good Hobbesian fashion at our inferiors, these hapless actors. But that's also what the Duke and his friends do. Bottom's company is here at their request, and has doubtless been paid a modest fee for the chance to play before such an elite crowd, even if the actors must endure the audience's barbs and demeaning wit as they stumble through the show.

Both the amateur actors in the inner play and the real-life actors portraying them must be convinced that they are serious performers committed to their craft. Bottom, as we know from an earlier scene, judges his acting as "lofty,"[19] and only worries that his performance will be too effective and drive the audience to an embarrassing onslaught of tears. The real-life actors must have this same confidence and dedication, although they anticipate laughter instead of tears, a parody of the theatre rather than a mournful tragedy of young love. Here, our superiority is confined to the fact that we know it is all a play, that we are watching good actors impersonate bad actors who are mercifully unaware of their mediocrity. Thus, our laughter is more disinterested, more aesthetic, "relaxed," as that term was defined in Chapter 5.

This dualism extends to the notion of two competing scripts, advanced by Kant and Raskin,[20] when Snout, playing Wall, steps out of character to explain his role to the onstage audience and then offers a preview of the tragic story. Moving in and out of character, he sees no irony in his double role, even taking Demetrius's funny and sarcastic line "It is the wittiest partition that ever I heard"[21] as high praise. We are reminded again of these competing scripts when the audience voices our own dismay at these rank amateurs, who, against all reason, fashion themselves as skilled actors. Any vestiges of the serious, of that potential Romeo and Juliet clouding the opening scene, are now gone, overwhelmed by these comically competing scripts providing an ironic link between on- and offstage and the real actors.

And then there's Wall. Directors have customarily indicated the chink by the actor's separating his fingers. But what would be the comic effect if, instead, he spreads his legs wide apart, like a Jumping Jack? Pyramus and Thisbe kneel on the floor, whispering through his legs.[22] This position visually reinforces the sexual allusions in lines directed at Wall: Bottom's "Cursed be thy stones" and Thisbe's "My cherry lips have often kissed thy stones." As Thisbe leans forward, her face just inches away from Bottom's on the other side, her lips puckered with an anticipated kiss, she cries out, "I kiss the wall's hole, not your lips at all." To get the gross double meaning, the two lovers can turn Wall around after Bottom's initial "stones," then once again to set up Thisbe's reference to the "wall's hole."

In the midst of all this, Bottom offers a second instance of competing scripts when he steps out of character to respond to Theseus's wanting the Wall to "curse again," assuring the Duke that the actor will come on his own cue, "Cursed be thy stones for thus deceiving me," the line now serving as both a gross joke and an unintentionally comic metadramatic aside from an actor breaking character.

Never has a company member so overestimated an audience's reaction as does Snug, proud of his effective roaring, in assuring the ladies that he is not really a lion. At the same time, these actors underestimate the audience's imaginative collaboration in the performance by having to bring out members of the company dressed as Wall and as Moon.

At some point, then, the concept of competing scripts merges with that of incongruity, as the absurd and the serious, the imaginative and the unimaginative are slapped together.

The lovers, in professing their fidelity, compare themselves to such mythic figures as Limander and Helen, and, for good measure, Shafalus and Procrus. Have they been reading the same school primer on famous lovers, and now are eager to show off their newfound knowledge, even though this isn't in director Quince's script? As they compete in this name-dropping, they deliver their lines at opposite sides of Wall, a parody of the connection good actors seek in making eye contact with each other. Meanwhile, the "chink," which had given rise to testicular and anal humor, still stands. At this point, the audience experiences what has been called the free play of jokes and physical shtick, both verbal and visual, with no other purpose than getting laughs. Pyramus and Thisbe, let alone Romeo and his Juliet, are left far behind. We are, as actors like to say, "in the moment."

The "relaxation" Robert Latta spoke of goes even further with the death speeches.[23] In fact, we no longer need those cynical comments from the aristocrats. The emotions—dread, fear of the unknown, denial, anxiety, all the defenses and verbal strategies we would expend in real life to avoid or mitigate death—are here rechanneled, diffused by our laughter as Freud and others suggest. In a world that for Pyramus and Thisbe is ruled by cruel fate, comedy provides relief from what is otherwise terrifying or inevitable. We laugh at the lovers' double suicide, as we do not and cannot in *Romeo and Juliet*. One is reminded of the double meaning in the Renaissance on "die" as both sexual consummation— at the end of this derisory production, not one, but three couples will go to bed to consummate their marriages!—and physical death, which likewise runs rampant in the play. Given their theological abhorrence of suicide, the ultimate sin against the Maker, the audience in 1595 could also here laugh at what would be unthinkable outside the theatre.

Unconsciously bad acting is inseparable from the heartfelt emotion in the face of death exhibited by the unlucky lovers themselves. Bottom points to the moon in a wildly romantic gesture, sure that the happy time of his meeting with Thisbe draws near, only to do a double take when he spots the bloody scarf, which he takes as evidence of her being devoured by the lion. He then becomes the bathetic ham actor of those creaky tragedies like *Gorboduc* through which Shakespeare himself surely suffered when he first came to London, their maudlin dramatic verse later parodied by the master playwright in the Player's lines in *Hamlet* where he delivers Aeneas's speech to Dido on the death of Priam. Within the space of a few lines, a cry to the Fates and Furies is coupled with Pyramus's pet name for Thisbe, "dainty duck." The lion has "deflower'd" his love, like some rival lover who first took her virginity. The actor can have fun with his "left pap," as Pyramus, in his anxiety, first places the sword on his right breast, before remembering that his heart's on the other side. Nothing funnier than a botched or misdirected suicide. Bottom even corrects himself on a matter of verb tense, changing Thisbe's state from "is" to "was." With "Tongue, lose thy light," he watches his soul mount to the sky—does this literalist actually pull on his tongue as if to send it on its way too? After all, the actor playing Moon takes literally Bottom's invocation to the eternal night of death by exiting on "Moon, take thy flight."

Bottom's "die, die, die, die, die" is the protracted death cry of the ham actor who doesn't want to leave the stage. He can fall onto the floor, twitching with the early signs of rigor mortis, then stagger to his feet, only to fall again, and repeat the process until he has milked the situation for all its worth, and at length with piteous groans collapse reluctantly to the stage. This is where physical comedy exercises strengthen the actor's performance. The actor can draw this out, so Thisbe, impatient and eager to make her entrance, might improvise by crying out, "Die, for God's sake, man, just die!"

Not to be outdone, once she realizes Pyramus is dead, the actor playing Thisbe has a treasure chest of comic shtick to plunder. She can run her hand over his cold body, attempting to get a reaction from Bottom, if not from Pyramus, that would give the lie to his exaggerated death performance, or she could mime words by moving his lips on "Speak, speak," only to conclude he is "quite dumb." Might Thisbe deliver this line to the audience? When Bottom looks up at her, as if telling her to get on with it, she can pull down his eyelids, as one would household shades, or pinch his nose, then his cheeks, trying to throw off her fellow actor. Once convinced he's dead, or will not be attempting another Lazarus-like rise from the tomb, she challenges the arrogant lead actor with her own mannered acting, the death speech full of banal alliterations, her hands thrashing about for the Sisters Three to come take her life. She might even borrow Bottom's physical bit with his tongue on "Tongue, not a word" as she dies. What about her coming miraculously back to life for a private curtain call, to the dismay of her fellow actors standing just offstage, with "And, farewell, friends. Thus Thisbe ends: Adieu, adieu, adieu."

At such a moment, our laughter is simple and direct, based as it is on the incongruity between the two actors believing they are giving the performance of their lives and a flagrant example of bad overacting. Freud would be beaming. We have laughed at death, and laughed at fictive actors who have consciously done nothing to merit our applause, even as we applaud the real-life actors behind them who have made us laugh by taking seriously what we all know is the epitome of the nonserious.

* * *

In the next chapter, we move from Shakespeare to playwrights of our day and examine variations of the word "comedy": a farce, *One Man, Two Guvnors*; a physical comedy, *The Play That Goes Wrong*; the romantic or sentimental comedy, *Calendar Girls*; and *The Same Deep Water as Me*, a sociopolitical play. Along with evaluating the differences in style, dialogue, theme, and staging that four such comedies present, we also posit an alternative approach in each for the actor.

Notes

1 For commentary on acting in Shakespeare's time, see John H. Astington, *Actors and Acting in Shakespeare's Time: The Art of Stage Playing* (Cambridge: Cambridge University Press, 2010); Andrew Gurr, *The Shakespearean Stage 1574–1642* (Cambridge: Cambridge University Press, 2009); Jeremy Lopez, *Theatrical Convention and Audience Response in Early Modern Drama* (New York: Cambridge University Press, 2002); Alan C. Dessen, *Elizabethan Stage Conventions and Modern Interpreters* (Cambridge: Cambridge University Press, 1984); and Patrick Tucker, *Secrets of Acting Shakespeare: The Original Approach* (New York: Routledge, 2002).

2 William Shakespeare, *The Tempest*, in *Arden Shakespeare Complete Works*, rev. ed., ed. Ann Thompson, David Scott Kastan, and Richard Proudfoot (London: Bloomsbury Arden Shakespeare, 2011), 1078. Citations to Shakespeare's plays in the main text are abbreviated and numerical by act, scene, and line(s).

Many of the suggestions and options in this chapter for playing the comic characters and staging the comic situations in Shakespeare come from our own experience as director and actor in the plays, and hence we indicate the productions that were the source of such possible options in the following notes.

3 Shakespeare, *The Comedy of Errors*, in *Arden Shakespeare Complete Works*, 201–2.

4 Directed Sidney Homan, Hippodrome State Theatre, Gainesville, Florida, 1985.

5 See Sidney Homan, "A Director's Concept for *The Comedy of Errors*," in *Directing Shakespeare: A Scholar Onstage* (Athens: Ohio University Press, 2004), 31–48.

6 Shakespeare, *The Taming of the Shrew*, in *Arden Shakespeare Complete Works*, 1053.

7 Directed by Stephanie Dugan, Wright State University, Dayton, Ohio, Spring, 1996.

8 Directed by Brian Rhinehart, Thomas Center, Gainesville, Florida, 1996.

9 Shakespeare, *Twelfth Night*, in *Arden Shakespeare Complete Works*, 1194.

10 Production at the Acrosstown Repertory Theatre, Gainesville, Florida, 1997.

11 Shakespeare, *Twelfth Night*, 1201.

12 Shakespeare, *Much Ado about Nothing*, in *Arden Shakespeare Complete Works*, 932.

13 Ibid., 933.

14 Ibid.

15 Ibid.

16 Shakespeare, *A Midsummer Night's Dream*, in *Arden Shakespeare Complete Works*, 889–912. Production of *A Midsummer Night's Dream*, Florida Theater, Gainesville, Florida, January 1986. See also Sidney Homan, "Adapting *A Midsummer Night's Dream* for the Cast, Producer, and Theatre," in *Directing Shakespeare*, 73–86; and Sidney Homan, "What Do I Do Now? Directing *A Midsummer Night's Dream*," in *Shakespearean Illuminations: Essays in Honor of Marvin Rosenberg*, ed. Jay L. Halio and Hugh Richmond (Newark: University of Delaware Press, 1998), 279–96.

17 One of the best studies of *A Midsummer Night's Dream*, of the antithetical worlds of Athens and the forest, is David Young's *Something of Great Constancy: The Art of "A Midsummer Night's Dream"* (New Haven, CT: Yale University Press, 1966).

18 Shakespeare, *A Midsummer Night's Dream*, 909–11.

19 Ibid., 893.

20 Immanuel Kant, *Critique of Judgment*, in *The Philosophy of Laughter and Humor*, ed. John Morreall (Albany: State University of New York

Press, 1987), 47; Victor Raskin, *Semantic Mechanisms of Humor* (Dordrecht: Reidel, 1984), 107–14.

21 Shakespeare, *A Midsummer Night's Dream*, 909.
22 "An Evening with William Shakespeare." Directed by Sidney Homan, Acrosstown Repertory Theatre, Gainesville, Florida, November, 2009.
23 Robert L. Latta, *The Basic Humor Process: A Cognitive-Shift Theory and the Case against Incongruity* (Berlin: Mouton de Gruyter, 1999), 44.

8

THE ACTOR AND FOUR FORMS OF COMEDY

Here, we look at four recent comedies that together display a range—though not the full range—of what comedy can mean, the forms it can take, and the special demands each form makes on the comedic actor. We first look at a farce, Richard Bean's *One Man, Two Guvnors*,[1] the playwright's reworking of Carlo Goldoni's classic *The Servant of Two Masters* (1746). How does the actor get into the world of farce? What style of delivery does it call for? How does the actor balance the verbal and physical demands of a play like *One Man, Two Guvnors*?

We then turn to physical comedy in *The Play That Goes Wrong* by Henry Lewis, Jonathan Sayer, and Henry Shields,[2] in which sets collapse, characters are accidentally injured on stage, props refuse to stay put, actors forget lines, and a cast desperately tries but fails to conceal the things that go wrong from the audience. This exaggerated physical comedy is also about the theatre, and what happens when things don't go as planned and actors are asked to improvise.

In Tim Firth's *Calendar Girls*,[3] we encounter sentient or romantic comedy, here based on real-life events when members of the Rylstone and District Women's Institute (WI) posed nude for a calendar to raise money for a leukemia research fund. Our focus here is on how the actor establishes a character in the first scene, making an impression on the audience and "winning them" over, even as the actor, knowing the entire arc of the story, is layering in subtextual material that will blossom as the character progresses through the play. We look at eleven exchanges of dialogue in the opening scene between the actors playing Chris and Anne, to show how they can be at once in the moment and yet aware of potential developments of their characters.

Finally, we examine Nick Payne's *The Same Deep Water as Me*,[4] a social–political comedy about low-life lawyers and their clients operating in what has been called the scam of Britain's "compensation culture." Its humor dark, even savage, the comedy is a sociological study of Scorpion Claims, to which the desperate come and, in the second act, the court system that, in this case, perpetuates a fraudulent claim. We look at three interactions among the play's major characters, with a special focus on one character's subtext and the ways that it might influence his delivery. A vital question here for the actor is how to balance the character's own lack of a moral compass with the unjust materialistic system that fuels it. And how does the actor play an individual who is also a representative or symbol of a failed society?

Playing Farce

The "rule" of comedy that the actor must play a character who takes his world seriously applies most emphatically with a farce like Richard Bean's *One Man, Two Guvnors*, a "pure" comedy in the playwright's words, and itself an adaptation of Carlo Goldoni's more-than-250-year-old farce *The Servant of Two Masters*. To complicate the actors' take on characters who unwittingly must believe fully in their world, there are here only a few vestiges of their history before the opening scene, that historical and psychological subtext the actor might otherwise fashion to flesh out the role, or even bring to it his own real-life experience. Rather, Bean's characters are driven by what the Elizabethans would call a "humor"; a single trait that, in Shakespeare's day, was the product of an excess of one of the four basic elements: earth, water, fire, air. Bean draws on the stock character types of the *commedia dell'arte*: the *dottore* (the pompous scholar), the *pantalone* (the rich elderly merchant with a young wife), the *zanni* (the clown), or the *inamorato* (the lover), among others. Alan, the would-be actor with no talent, conflates everything about him with the theatre. Pauline is the daffy ingénue—in her lover Alan's words, "unspoiled by education, like a new bucket."[5] Dangle, the lawyer bound up in the contorted speech of legalisms. The use of these stereotypes is another barrier for the actor to overcome.

The characters inhabit a sphere with no center, much like the random world of quantum mechanics. Oh, there is a plot of sorts: disguised as her dead brother Roscoe (who was killed by her boyfriend Stanley Stubbers), Rachel comes to Brighton to collect £6,000 from the father of her fiancé. Francis serves both "Roscoe" and Stubbers, but must keep them apart to prevent discovery. The secondary characters—the lovers Pauline and Alan, Pauline's father Charlie Clench and his partner Lloyd Boateng, and various servants—revolve around this trinity. But the plot is a parody of a plot—a love affair between a sister and her brother's murderer, a voracious servant who serves two masters he has to keep apart on the same day in the same town (shades of Shakespeare's *The Comedy of Errors*)—but this plot is little more than a means to bring together characters separated by murder and fate. Even the pretentious actor Alan acknowledges that "character" is defined solely by "action."[6]

Thus, the actors play stock characters who go through their predestined paces unaware of their artificiality, consumed by their particular humor in a world that gives a twist to the notion of "the theatre of the absurd." They make jokes, most of them bad and strained; there are sudden improvisations, characters who confuse each other with the sound of a single word: Dangle toasts *ars amandi* ("the art of love") but Pauline thinks he's confused her with some anonymous "Mandy."[7] When Francis asks Lloyd if they "do sandwiches" at The Cricketers Arms, Charlie chastises him with "Wash your mouth out! It's a pub, that does food."[8] When Dangle asks if Roscoe Crabbe was "mortally wounded," Charlie counters with "No! He was killed."[9]

Actors must play them as earnest characters who think they use metaphors for the sake of clarifying an abstract situation. For the audience, the metaphors make no sense, the picture called up for illustration at odds with the thought behind the line. Alan is the main violator here. Insisting his love for Pauline is "pure," he likens it to "the kind of water you're supposed to put in a car battery";[10] fearing Roscoe has taken Pauline away from him, he speaks of his "dream" of their lost love as "dead ... like a discarded Russian astronaut dog landing on my head";[11] and, claiming he is "dangerous, unpredictable," and thus no longer responsible for his actions, he compares himself to "a wasp in a shop window."[12] Even Stanley succumbs: when Rachel asks him if he feels terrible for having "presumed that [she] must be Paddy's employer who died," he comes up with the puzzling, "I felt like a floral clock in the middle of winter." Still, the simile makes sense to Rachel: "That's exactly how I felt! All the flowers dead." Then the lovers proceed to run it into the ground. Rachel elaborates on his "And yet the mechanism of the clock is pointlessly turning" with "the hour hand pointing to a dead geranium," and, not to be outdone, Stanley adds, "The minute hand stuck on a long gone begonia."[13] Make sense of this who can, but it is not nonsense to the two characters. The actors need to "wrap their collective heads" around this exchange to make sense of it for the audience.

The farce can be as physically exhausting as it is verbally. In Act One, Scene Four, Francis tries to keep Rachel and Stanley apart by confining his two masters in separate rooms facing each other with only an *"aperitif bar squeezed between"* them.[14] Orders for food are delivered to the wrong party, and the comedy gets rough when the aged assistant waiter Alfie falls down a flight of stairs when Francis lifts a tureen off his tray and *"overbalances"* the old man.[15] Moments later, when standing *"on the two handles of the cork screw,"* as Alfie pulls at it, *"the cork releases and he knocks himself out."*[16]

Again, for the characters, their world is logical, their metaphors spot on. Act Two, Scene Three, takes this trust to its inevitable conclusion when they fall into a wild battle for alliteration with the letter *"d"* as they discuss they the cause of Paddy's death, a fictitious character invented by Francis:

Stanley [*hearing that Francis got a framed photo from Paddy before he died*]   Before he did ... before he did what?
Francis Before he did . . . die.
Stanley He did die did he?
Francis He did.
Stanley What did he die of?
Francis He was diagnosed with diarrhea but died of diabetes.
Stanley He died of diabetes did he?
Francis He did didn't he.[17]

(Act Two, Scene Three)

This may look like an acting exercise to loosen the tongue but, for the two characters, it is no such thing—and it is deadly serious. Two pages later in the script, when Francis talks with Rachel, the *"d"* words will expand to include dorking, diaphragm, duck, directly, daft, and definitely.[18]

Even as Act One accustoms (perhaps inculcates) the audience to this wild farce of linguistic overkill, fractured metaphors, and what, from our perspective, can only be described as mindless alliteration, the play brings in new characters, a collage of *dei ex machina* who only aggravate the situation: a vicar, an old woman, a taxi driver, and a policeman. Two volunteers from the audience are asked to come on stage and are "*taught correct ... lifting technique*" so they can carry Stanley's trunk into the pub.[19] Cautioning Pauline that Alan may not deserve her love, Dolly tells women in the house, "Don't take notes girls, there's a handout at the end."[20] When Francis asks them "What's a good first date from the girl's point of view?"[21] the actor is told that "*This is an opportunity for improvisation*," and when he rejects the playwright's suggestion of "*dinner, theatre, whatever*," Dolly agrees to his weird idea of going on "a rabbit shoot," albeit adding, "And maybe we could go to dinner afterwards."[22]

The earlier reference to the random universe of quantum mechanics where the laws of physics are no longer applicable and things can happen without a clear cause well describes the final expansion of the world of *One Man, Two Guvnors* as it swallows up the theatre itself. The seemingly confined stage world of farce dissolves as the characters become metadramatic critics without realizing it. By invoking the theatre as they try to make sense of the situation, they only remind us that we are watching a play, and we are at once involved and yet uninvolved in a double bind that would have won Brecht's approval.

This is perhaps the actors' greatest challenge in *One Man, Two Guvnors*: despite using language and metaphors based on the theatre and the very profession of the actor, they are blissfully unaware of being in a play and hence at the greatest remove from the audience. What we see as fake, an illusion, they see as real, even as they now use theatre-based metaphors that are actually more relevant than the fractured nontheatrical metaphors they use elsewhere. Alan derides an arranged marriage as "worthy of a Molière farce."[23] He justifies changing his name from Orlando to Alan on the grounds that "Actors' Equity already had an Orlando Dangle," and, besides, "It's 1963, there's a bloody revolution in the theatre and angry young men are writing plays about Alans."[24] Rachel predicts that one day "everyone will have their own telephone that they carry around with them" but worries that the futuristic device "might ring in the theatre."[25] A director might be tempted to have a real phone ring here on cue! Charlie is sure that Alan won't stab "Roscoe" with the knife bought—of all places—at Woolworths since "this is real, it ain't a play."[26]

It is interesting that, among all these characters using theatrical references and figures of speech innocently and yet prophetically, Francis and Dolly, the two servants, are the only ones who suspect what is going on—in effect, seeing the play for what it is and thinking of the audience as an audience, rather than as extras to be dragged into the story. Francis tell us "this play is based on Carlo Goldoni's two-hundred-year-old Italian comedy *A Servant of Two Masters*," identifies himself ("that's me") as "the Harlequin," and then raises the question of what "motivation" he'll have in the second act since he "has now eaten."[27] Dolly, as we have seen, addresses the audience both directly and through asides, and often provides a psychological gloss for the other characters, as when she tells us that Alan "wants to be an actor."[28] Their sense of the theatre and their concomitant identification with those in the house may be part of the convention in such comedies that the servants are wiser than the masters.

To be sure, there are references to reality outside the farce's hermetically sealed world: Rachel mentions Australia as offering a "terrible outdoorsie life, sustained by lager, barbecues, and opera";[29] Stanley dismisses Charlie's boast that his lawyer friend Dangle "got the Mau Mau off" with "But in Kenya the Mau Mau killed a hundred thousand innocent men, women, and children."[30] For the actor, the mention of Canada or Kenya might let them open a thin beam of light into characters otherwise indifferent to anything outside what they take as reality. Or perhaps Pauline, beautiful but not very bright, acts aghast at the suggestion of relocating to Australia because this is what she's heard from more sophisticated people. And nowhere else in the play does Stanley show any political interest, let alone concern with anyone else except himself.

However, there is one curious, and seemingly irrelevant, even digressive moment in the play wherein Francis and Dolly—appropriately—go on for two pages of dialogue about a topic that appears to have no place in the farce: how to build a petrol station.[31] Alone onstage with Dolly, Francis boasts that men "don't just walk into things with [their] eyes closed" as women do. Dolly in turn delivers an aside, a silent "*look*" to the audience as if to signal something interesting, perhaps even significant is about to happen. The subject is initiated by Francis's fractured metaphor comparing the "planning" that successful love requires to "building a new petrol station." He insists that you need to sink the petrol reservoirs before building the shop—that is, the major purpose of the station is selling gas, while the sort of stuff you'd buy in the convenience store is secondary. Dolly argues that, as you don't build the shop "directly on top of the reservoirs," what difference does it make? The actors might be tempted to identify the petrol reservoirs with the male, the shop with the female. But, while there might be something moderately funny in the lovers' clash of genders, what function can the ensuing argument have? Francis gives a four-step schedule for building the station, insisting that it would make no sense—it would be "brainless," like a woman—to build the shop first, as you'd only have to tear it down to sink in the reservoirs. Dolly offers a woman's schedule: making sure there is enough land "so you could factor in a pleasant walk from the pump, to the shop," adding "a bit of lawn," along with flowers, a rookery, and "somewhere for the kids to play." The argument is resolved, at least for the time being, when they get to the issue of toilets: Dolly insists on a "nice" station, with separate toilets for women with three times as many stalls as the men's. But, after Francis truculently insists that "nobody in their right mind wants petrol stations to be nice," and links their present argument to the conflict between men and women, between "Me and you," Dolly lets out a single, anguished "No," and Francis suddenly capitulates, confessing his love: "That's a shame. 'Cause I really fancy you." It's as if this brief excursion into the real world, the building of petrol stations, grubby or nice, the argument over priorities, only serves to hurtle the characters back into the play at hand.

Later, Francis gets Stanley to buy Dolly a ticket to Spain, and then, warning him that she should not go alone into that land of over-amorous men, convinces him to throw in "another fifty" so he can go with her.[32] He has already assured the audience that, having met his objective in Act One (where he was "driven by [his] animal urges, hunger"), he has now found an actor's objective for the second act: "because I've eaten, I am humanized, civilized, and I can embrace the potential of love."[33]

Even while seducing the most serious, sober-minded, even humorless spectator to laugh as the comedy mocks, upturns, challenges our world offstage, this farce is about something and thereby more than a running joke.

Physical Comedy

The Play That Goes Wrong is really two plays, both of which are plagued by accidents, errors, misinterpretations, and misunderstandings. One is a generic murder mystery—"Murder at Haversham Manor," a production of the totally inept Cornley Polytechnic Drama Society—coexisting with a second play. Real-life actors play actors playing characters in the murder mystery, and, when we refer to them, we will use both the actor's and the character's name—hence, Sandra/"Florence" or Max/ "Cecil Haversham."

With the best of intentions, reviewers have tended to praise the play as "pure fun," fun for the sake of fun.[34] But, how should the actor make that character as "human" as possible to produce laughter that is not just superficial? What are the ranges of physical comedy that the actor must master? How does the actor stay in character—indeed, stay in two, even if complementary, characters?

Let's look first at some examples of the range of the play's physical comedy.

Obstacles

The obstacles in this play are literal, part of the set. At the top of the show, Annie/the stage manager is seen kneeling by the fireplace *"trying to attach a mantelpiece to it."*[35] Realizing she can't *"hold it and nail at the same time,"* in her desperation, she calls on someone in the audience to come up and help.[36] Obstacles are also moveable, to a comic degree: handcuffed to the chaise longue, but ordered by Jonathan/"Charles" to fetch papers from what once was the second-floor study, Dennis/"Perkins" must drag himself and the heavy piece of furniture across the stage.

Entrance and Exit Problems

Just getting on or off the stage presents an obstacle. Attempting to go through a door that won't budge, Robert/"Thomas" is forced to dart around the side of the set to enter the set. Even the well-worn theatrical term "taking the stage" gets an ironic twist when Sandra/"Florence" can't go through the same inoperable door, and, in desperation, makes her first appearance in the window, caught holding apart the curtains in that twilight zone between on- and offstage. Falling on the floor when the canvas on the stretcher with which Robert/"Thomas" and Dennis/ "Perkins" would have carried him offstage breaks, Jonathan/"Charles," though "dead," but realizing he was meant to have been carried off, *"slowly starts to get up trying not to be seen"* and manages a clumsy exit *"dragging the stretcher canvas with him."*[37]

Accidents

When Chris/"Inspector Carter" arrives, the heraldic shield above the door falls down, hitting him in the face; good member of the company as he is and with no shame in breaking the illusion, he rehangs the offending object. When Sandra/"Florence" is hit by the door as Robert/"Thomas" bursts in, followed by Max/"Cecil," and knocked unconscious, the "accident" presents two problems: unconscious, possibly badly hurt, she must be removed from the stage; and she will later fume when Annie/stage manager, her rival and with no acting ability, takes over the part, script in hand. Sandra/"Florence" revives in the second act only to be knocked out again when Max/"Cecil," resisting her attempt at seduction, pushes her into the clock, as Trevor, inside, knocks her out again when he opens the clock door. Sandra/"Florence" is placed on the chaise longue while Trevor/lighting and sound operator, no better than Annie/stage manager at acting, takes over her part with "But I'm a beautiful woman, how can you resist me?"[38]

Misplaced Props

There is a series of wildly misplaced props when Robert/"Thomas," failing to find a pencil for the Inspector, substitutes a key. Dennis/ "Perkins," searching for keys to lock all the residents inside the manor for their own safety, is forced to use the Inspector's notebook instead, and, ten lines later, Robert/"Thomas," coming to fetch the now-missing notebook, picks up a vase on his exit. The comic routine is reborn a page later when Chris/"Inspector Carter" asks for his pencil and Robert/ "Thomas" produces the keys, and then offers him the vase when the

Inspector asks for his notebook. The most disastrous misplaced prop comes when Annie/stage manager, with the best of intentions, leans through the upstage window to exchange an empty bottle of scotch (which Dennis/"Perkins" tries to pretend is full) with one filled with "white spirit" whose vintage the butler announces as "Flammable and corrosive, sir."[39]

The Unstable Set

If Act One had problems with props, set problems grow by a quantum leap in Act Two—something of a physical arc for the comedy. The bottom of the elevator leading to the top floor study breaks; summoned by Chris/"Inspector Carter," Robert/"Thomas" tries to climb to the upper level. When the upper level drops a second time, *"putting it on even more of an incline,"*[40] the desk comes sliding toward Robert/"Thomas," who stops it but is now stuck holding all of the furniture. When the upper level fully collapses, crushing Trevor/lighting and sound operator, the disaster is capped by a witty observation from Robert/"Thomas" to Chris/"Inspector Carter": "I don't think they noticed."[41]

In the closing moments, there is total chaos with the set. Jonathan/"Charles" *"bursts in through the upper-level door, falls off the edge, grabs on to the broken truss and swings across the stage,"* sending three fellow actors/characters *"flying."*[42] At the end, Dennis/"Perkins," still dragging the chaise longue, knocks over the door flat. Chris/"Inspector Carter" just gets out of the way of the falling flat, while Robert/"Thomas" collides with the fireplace flat, leveling it and *"leaving Annie standing in the window frame and revealing Sandra dazed backstage."*[43] In the silence, Max/"Cecil" throws some artificial snow from offstage. In the closing moments, as Robert/"Thomas," the guilty brother, dies, Jonathan/"Charles" comes forward to draw a moral from the play that is out of left field: "If men allow their conscience to be governed by avarice then death and destruction shall prevail"—said *"with finality."*[44] As he closes the play with "Let us hope we never again see a murder at Haversham Manor," there is a blackout *"just before [a falling chandelier] hits him."*[45]

Improvised Dialogue, Role Reversals, and Script Problems

All this physical comedy has an inevitable effect on the dialogue, as the actors must constantly improvise. When Sandra/"Florence" forgets her cue for Chris/"Inspector Carter" to read her letter to her lover, he is forced to mime her line with a *"high voice"* — "You've read my letter? Where did you find it?" — and then answer himself (*"back to his normal voice"*) with "I'll tell you where I found it! In Charles' pocket!"[46] Forced to take the part of Sandra/"Florence", Annie/stage manager ends Act One mistakenly reading a direction to the lighting designer: "This is a disaster! Blackout. Interval," then corrects herself with an "Oh!" — we cannot be sure if that "Oh!" punctuates "disaster" or acknowledges her mistake as a character in calling for a blackout.[47] Earlier, when she trips, scattering the script to the floor, she tries to pick up the pages, but they are out of order, and, with no skill at improvisation, she can only repeat the line she said before the accident: "Oh, the tension in this house is … Oh, the tension in this … oh, it … oh, it's tense."[48] When Robert/"Thomas" tries to come to her aid with "Florence. How are you feeling now?" his offer only leads to her uninspired ad lib, "I'm good, yeah, really good."[49]

No two actors charged with playing, say, Chris/"Inspector Carter" in separate productions will give the exact same performance, but, instead, will invariably bring to the play their own individual comic style, routines, and shtick that worked in previous shows.

Sentimental or Romantic Comedy

The advice given to someone applying for a job — "Make a good first impression" — applies, in a unique way, to the actor appearing in the first scene of a comedy. Taking the meaning of "impress" in its more literal sense (i.e., applying a seal by bearing down on the wax so it makes a mark), the actor needs to *impress* the audience. You need to establish your character not only with such dialogue as the playwright gives you, but also in that subtext you devise — the character's history, what the character is thinking and feeling beneath the lines, his or her inner voice, and — so important — the objective, the end: what the character wants.

That goal is there in the beginning, from the first scene, although the character is still embryonic. Conversely, the actor doesn't start with a blank slate, as he knows the ending and can use that information to heighten the comedy. The opening of Harold Pinter's *The Lover*[50] demonstrates this point well. The actors know the husband is also the lover, the couple's way of spicing up a marriage while remaining faithful to each other. The audience doesn't—until Max appears halfway through the play. So, the comedy here rests on a double subtext:

Richard (*amiably*)   Is your lover coming today?

Sarah Mmnn.

Richard What time?

Sarah Three.

Richard Will you be going out ... or staying in?

Sarah Oh ... I think we'll stay in.

Richard I thought you wanted to go to that exhibition.

Sarah I did, yes ... but I think I'd prefer to stay in with him today.

Richard Mmn-hmmn. Well, I must be off.

He goes to the hall and puts on his bowler hat.

Richard Will he be staying long do you think?

Sarah Mmmnnn . . .

Richard About ... six, then.

Sarah Yes.

Richard Have a pleasant afternoon.

Sarah Mmnn.

Richard Bye-bye.

Sarah Bye.[51]

Richard, whose jealousy for Max is apparent here, knows he is actually jealous of himself, of the other role he's playing. But, while making sure the audience senses the jealousy, the actor must conceal the truth, only letting a touch of this other self rise briefly to the surface. As a director, we have seen varied responses when Max does appear. Some audience members are totally surprised—they never suspected this, thinking, instead, that they were going to see a standard comedy of adultery. Others said they had their suspicions, however dim, confirmed. And still others had figured it out from the start—or claimed they did.

Tim Firth's *Calendar Girls* presents the range of comedy running through the play in the first scene: one liners, witty exchanges, parodies of characters slightly off-center (such as Marie, the director, and Brenda Hulse, the guest speaker), the horseplay, and joyous mock battles to which the characters of the village's WI are peculiarly susceptible, and even the use of humor as a defense against the darker aspects of their lives. Not a farce and not especially given to physical humor, *Calendar Girls* is perhaps best described as a sentimental or bittersweet comedy. The audience will also come to the performance somewhat prepared as the story is based on that of eleven real-life WI members who, as the play's back cover notes, "posed nude for a calendar to raise money for the Leukaemia Research Fund."[52]

In the style of George Bernard Shaw, who often gave lengthy portraits of a character just before their first line, Firth has provided notes on the play's central figures, Chris and Annie. Chris is the type of person you "want … at your party." She is "at home in crowds" and loves "being the centre of attention." Then he adds, "Without Chris in her life, Annie would be better behaved, her life less fun." Annie is "at heart more conformist and less confrontational than Chris." But, as Chris "saves Annie from being a saint," she has "enough edge to be interesting, and enough salt not to be too sweet." Then he makes a link between the two that is essential to our analysis: "Together these two are greater than the sum of their parts … Each is spiritual mustard to the other's meat."[53]

In the first scene of *Calendar Girls*, the actors playing Annie and Chris can start impressing the audience, even as they layer in their larger knowledge of the characters. Annie and Chris, this is to say, are not static but will evolve; still, the actors will want to underscore from the start, even if the words the playwright offers are minimal, those dimensions of their characters that will bear fruit as the play moves forward. The setting for this opening scene is the church hall in Knapeley village. The women have gathered for a WI meeting, incorporating some choral singing, and then a tai chi lesson from Chris. We will examine ten discrete moments that bring Annie and Chris together, both as characters and actors, and raise some challenges, questions, or options in terms of approaches the actors might take, all focused on the way the play's end is configured in its beginning.

1. Annie accuses Chris of never having read the book on tai chi she bought her, of simply making "it all up." Insisting she has read the book "cover to cover," Chris mocks Annie by suggesting a tai chi movement she calls "Annie, Sharing Her Maltesers with Her Best Friend in the Cinema": she mimes "*A rugby-style hand-off with her left hand, whilst repeatedly squirreling mouthfuls from an imaginary pot with her right.*" Annie brands this a "lie," insisting she has "*always* let [Chris] have some."[54]

Chris's tai chi exercises clash comically with the formal atmosphere of the church hall, established here in the darkness by a "solo female voice" (Cora's) singing the WI anthem "Jerusalem." But, knowing the ultimate quarrel between the women, when Annie will later accuse Chris of using the nude calendar not for the memory of her husband John but to stoke her own ego, her own need to take the spotlight, will the two actors want to suggest subtextually a deeper division between Annie and Chris? Annie may fear that Chris's ego will violate their friendship. Chris fears that Annie is right, a suspicion that she tries to dismiss through parody. This means that the actors can take their actions a bit over the top, make their feelings behind the exercises a bit more blatant. It's not just about knowing the plot, where the play is going; it's about using that to enhance the comedy, the action, to bring the characters more to the front for the audience.

2. When Marie, the director of the WI, turns on Chris for not bringing the flowers she promised for this evening's speaker, Chris pleads that, while she and her husband Rod normally have leftovers, this time they were in no "position to turn down any sales." But when Marie exits petulantly, insisting "you *promise* these things, Chris, and you don't deliver," Annie "(*nodding to Chris*)" interjects, "You could put that on the side of your van. 'Harper's Florists—we promise but we don't deliver.' "[55]

Chris has two problems, with her husband and with their dying business; relatively minor, to be sure, compared to Annie's problem with a dying husband. Both dislike the officious chairman, Marie— they can bond on that. So, Annie's play on "promise" and "deliver" is meant to be funny, using Marie's petulant complaint as a slogan for the flower shop. Her real object, then, is Marie, as she comes to the aid of her friend through sarcasm. But, given Chris's business and marital problems, does Annie's joke, albeit well-intended, cut deeper? Chris will later choose a TV contract and the chance to appear in a commercial for "washing powder" over helping her husband's business at the Northern Bridal Fair. Marie's complaint, then, may inadvertently touch on a personal failing of Chris, one that will threaten the friendship of the very woman now coming to her aid. The possibility here seems at once thematic and yet also of psychological value for the actor.

3. Fearing Chris, as usual, will make fun of tonight's speaker—who last year presented, as Marie recalls, "a fascinating talk on the history of the tea towel"[56]—there is the following quick exchange between Annie and Chris:

> **Annie** (*to Chris*)   Now just shut up, OK. Whatever this is, you just shut up. I only laugh 'cause you laugh.
> **Chris** I'm not going to laugh.
> **Annie** No, you say that every time and then you laugh and it's ME that gets into trouble. You have to *promise* me—
> **Chris** (*dead serious*)   I am not going to laugh.[57]

(Act One, Scene One)

Sure, both the speaker and her topic are comic, absurd—the sort of senseless event that, until the nude calendar, defines the activities of the WI members. But, for better or worse, note that Annie is more concerned about proper social behavior, even in the presence of a fool like Brenda Hulse. She senses both the virtue (Chris makes her laugh) and the danger of their friendship (Annie is the one who gets into trouble). And note also that the word "promise" comes back in their exchange. The playwright describes Chris's reply as *"dead serious."* Has Annie's outburst, which Chris cuts off, resonated deeper within her?

4. Brenda's topic tonight is to be "the fascinating world . . . of broccoli," but when the projector *"cuts out with a bang"* and she insists she can't go on without her slides, there is the following exchange between Chris and Annie:

> **Chris** (*feigning despair*)   Oh God DAMMIT.
> **Annie** (*crying, hand over face*)   Stop it-t . . .[58]

(Act One, Scene One)

No problem with Chris's sarcasm, but what about Annie? One actor took her *"crying, hand over face"* as laughing so hard at Chris that she starts to cry, and therefore tries to cover her reaction. But another took the gesture as a serious concern even for a silly person like Brenda, and embarrassment at her friend Chris, who just minutes before had promised not to laugh. If one response promotes the comedy and the other the friendship, how does an actor choose?

5. When Marie proposes as a general topic next year's calendar and "the twelve most beautiful views—," Chris cuts her off by saying "*privately to Annie*":

Chris Of George Clooney.
Marie (*approaching the end of her tether*)—of Wharfedale
    Bridges, with—
Chris Eleven fully-clothed with a little "lift-the-flap" for December.
Chris *capitalizes on this to* **Annie**. **Marie** *advances on* **Chris**.[59]

(Act One, Scene One)

Here, of course, is the joke that will lead to the idea of the WI's nude calendar to raise money for John's memorial. Annie has no lines, but what reaction will the actor choose? Is she interested, even intrigued by the idea of a nude calendar? Or concerned that, once again, Chris is making fun of someone who, however fatuous, means well? Should Chris mime lifting the flap, looking lustfully at an imaginary nude George Clooney? Does she take Annie's silence as a sign that she's no longer resisting Chris, is being drawn into her world, one where sex, money, and a good deed are inextricably mixed? It's notable that Firth used the word "*capitalizes*" in the stage direction for his actor playing Chris. To the director and the actor, this indicates the character should again make the moment larger.

These moments constitute a sort of "dance" between the two main characters of attraction and hesitation, a bonding in which friendship is often expressed through humor at the other's expense, yet a connection that is also fragile. Surrounded by other characters whose pasts, once revealed, become a factor in the "group dynamics" of the six WI members, this dance between Annie and Chris constitutes, structurally, the scene's first half. John's entrance will add a new dimension, making the comedy more poignant, undermining the jokes and that joyous horseplay concealing a darker level, and turning it into what we might call a tragicomedy.

6. Regarding Celia's "I have to say your man's looking VERY chiseled these days. (*To John*) Not got you on a health kick, has she?" "*Annie and Chris make eye contact,*"[60] again, there's a choice for the actors here. We will assume all the women know of John's cancer, though not the latest diagnosis. So Celia tries a bit of ribbing, a joke that passes off John's condition as a "health kick." But what do the actors make of the "*eye contact*" between Annie and Chris? Again, there are options for the actors: they are touched by Celia's attempt to lighten the situation; the joke falls flat when they see John wince; given what Annie knows, suspects, or fears, the well-intentioned "health kick" is sadly, even absurdly, inadequate, and she conveys this to Chris. In light of that "dance" of the first five moments, perhaps Annie and Chris are one here, linked by seeing themselves in the other, as the existentialists would say. This is a union that will be tested in Act Two.

7. Following Jesse's lines to John: "You *have* lost weight. Your *cheeks* are really looking—."

Chris (*leaping in*)   God I wish y'd have a word with my Rod. He's getting a right old paunch.
Annie (*putting her arms round* **John**)   Works too hard, that's his problem.[61]

(Act One, Scene One)

Whatever faults or character flaws Chris may have, here she is Annie's "champion," trying to erase the well-meant, honest, but unintentionally caustic pronouncement by deflecting the reference to her husband. Then Annie tries to stave off any further harm by putting her arms around John and blaming the weight loss on the fact that he works too hard. For staging, what about having Annie and Chris on either side of John, as a trinity confronting Celia and Jessie, good souls but stepping into dangerous waters here?

8. For a moment, Annie and Chris are alone:

Annie Thanks for that.
Chris No, really. He does look good, I wasn't just saying.
Annie Yes. Well.
Chris *touches* **Annie**'s *hair, like she probably did when they were in their twenties.*

Chris When's he due in the doctor's?

Annie We go Friday.

The notion of "fingers being crossed" is in the air between these two old mates.[62]

(Act One, Scene One)

In this moving exchange between *"two old mates,"* the twin poles of *Calendar Girls*, life and death, are firmly established for the audience. As the play fluctuates between the characters, it underscores the ways comedy and tragedy complement and heighten one another.

9. It's Chris who offers sunflower seeds to John on the condition that he come back and give a talk to the WI. When he declines, she threatens to throw away the seeds, until he rescues them by promising to do so, and then shows the women how to toast the seeds—"little parcels of sunlight," as he calls them—the result being that, if you eat one, it "turns your mouth into liquid Yorkshire."[63]

Annie is silent during this exchange, but she knows that Chris knows the sad context of her friend's gift of the sunflower seeds and her empty threat to throw them away if he does not come back to address the women. There is, then, a special, "silent" conversation between the two women, especially if the other four characters (Cora, Celia, Jessie, and Ruth) are not fully appraised of his condition. It is undoubtedly more difficult to stand on stage without any lines than to be part of the dialogue. She must play this poignant scene with austerity.

10. At the end of the scene, as Annie chides John for not taking her with him to the doctors and then tries to raise his spirits by *"telling him the answer she wants to hear,"* the conversation is interrupted when Chris appears in the doorway. As John goes out to join the drinkers, Chris *"knows in a micro-second something's wrong."*[64]

Chris What's the matter?

Annie (*beat, then on autopilot*) I'm fine.

Chris I have not put up with you for four hundred years to be batted off with an "I'm fine."

Annie *takes her time.*

Annie John's got his results.

> **Chris** *doesn't have to ask further. After twenty-nine years "putting up," she doesn't need telling. She just goes to her oldest friend and holds her. [Then]* **Chris** *guides* **Annie** *out.*[65]

(Act One, Scene One)

The touching, emotional exchange pushes the comedy offstage, and thus completes the arc of the first scene, from the petty, good-natured (though revealing) quarrels of Annie and Chris, to the WI's witty conflict with Marie, and the parody of the guest speaker in Brenda—the humor ranging from innocent to bawdy to sarcastic.

Actors and directors speak of "playing the moment" or "being in the moment." The analysis of these ten such moments between Annie and Chris illustrate and encourage just that. Playing the tragedy behind the comedy is one of the oldest theatre traditions, and here Firth gives the actors opportunity to use their talents to show this. At times, they must appear oblivious to the tragic elements and simply set free the comedy.

Social Comedy

In *The Same Deep Water as Me*, two solicitors, Andrew and Barry, in their failing law firm, Scorpion Claims, take on Kevin Needleman as a client and file a fraudulent accident report, wherein Kevin, his wife Jennifer (Andrew's former girlfriend), and their child fake being victims of a car crash involving a Tesco company van. This scam occupies the first act. Andrew assures Kevin that the defendants will settle the case out of court. In the second act, when the case does surprisingly go to court, the Needlemans, grilled by Tesco's sharp lawyer, give conflicting and disastrous testimonies. Still, the judge rules in the Needlemans' favor, and this leads to Kevin joining the two lawyers in filing a series of fraudulent claims. At the end, there's a fight between Andrew and Kevin, the partnership is dissolved, and the play concludes with a bittersweet scene (which we will examine below) between Andrew and Jennifer, who may be leaving Kevin.

Here, following, is an exchange in which Andrew and Barry voice conflicting objectives, each trying to overcome an obstacle presented by his partner: Barry refusing to take on Kevin's fraudulent case

(Jennifer and their child weren't even in the car at the time of the staged accident), Andrew trying to convince his partner to do just that. Each has a strong need to win the other over to his point of view in a clash of legal ethics and practicality. This inseparable link between objective and obstacle plays out in five stages, as noted below, with each followed by some questions the actor might want to consider.

Andrew Why y'calling him?

Barry Tell him he can shove his claims up his fucking—

Andrew Why?

Barry You stoned or some'ing? 'S bullshit, 's a bullshit claim.

Andrew So?

Barry So we're not going near it.

Andrew Why not?

Barry Because 's fraud.

Andrew Never bothered you before.

Barry Fuck's that s'posed t' mean?

Andrew I'm just saying, Barry.

Barry Now hang on a minute; I have never knowingly—

Andrew Ah, bullshit. Arthur Garfield ring any bells?

Barry Fuck you on about?

Andrew ... Antonio DeSilva, Michael Pakulshi, thingy Patel, Will Baker—

Barry There may have been times when I had a creeping suspicion that—

Andrew "Creeping suspicion?"

Barry ... one or two minor elements of a particular claim—

Andrew "One or two minor elements"—Jesus Christ, Barry, we took on a woman who reckoned her boobs exploded.

Barry *One* of her boobs. That was a legitimate—

Andrew Listen I have thought about this and I have thought about this and you wanna know how I feel about it?

Barry What d'ya mean, you've thought about it?

Andrew Who gives a fuck if some behemoth of an insurance company, who look after one of the biggest supermarket chains in the—

Barry What d'ya mean you've—

Andrew Who, by the way, probably don't even pay their—

Barry Wha d'ya mean, you've thought about it, how have y'thought about it? Motherfucker only juss told us.

Andrew I'm saying in the abstract.

Barry No y'not.

Andrew Oh come off it, Barry, give me some fucking credit. You think if I had anything to do with that weaselly motherfucker and his drop-in-the-ocean claim I wouldn't've spruced it up a bit?—

Barry Who said anything about—

Andrew I'm saying generally speaking. There is a culture. That exits. And whether you or I like it or not—

Barry This is my firm.

Andrew Sorry t' have t' be the one to break it to ya, Barry, only reason 's your firm is cos the bloke who used to run it died.

Barry 'S also the only reason you've not out of a fucking job, so show a bit o' respect.[66]

(Act One)

Objective–Obstacle: Stage One

Here, once Barry realizes Andrew wants to take on Kevin as a client, he asserts himself in the most graphic way possible: "Tell him he can shove his claim up his fucking—" and then underscores his position by suggesting his partner must be "stoned or some'ing." All Andrew can do is counter with a few equivocal words—"So," "Why not."

Questions for the Actors

Do you want to play the moment here, confining the "history" of the two characters to what we know of them in the play? Or invent a history for each—a childhood in which, say, confronted by an accuser on the playground, each had a different way of responding?

What's their posture, where are they standing onstage as this "fight" begins? Does Andrew move toward Barry threateningly on his "Why not?" Or, does he back off—perhaps because he knows the answer ("fraud"). He's heard it before.

How does each balance what we cited in Chapter 3 as "external needs" (especially in the more ethically conscious Barry) and "external necessity" (Andrew's fear that Scorpion Claims is failing and needs Kevin's "business")?

Objective–Obstacle: Stage Two

Now Andrew tries to take over, reminding Barry he's violated this self-righteous stance in the past. Lawyer-like, he rattles off a series of clients whose suits were less than genuine. Barry admits only that he had a "creeping suspicion," but just about minor items. Getting specific, Andrew wins this round by citing the woman who wanted to sue because her fake breasts exploded. This time it's Barry who plays the literalist lawyer: it was only "*one* of her boobs." From the audience's perspective, this parody of legalese arguments and counterarguments is crude and comic—exploding breasts, whether two or one, along with the hair-splitting quibble of "creeping suspicion." But not, of course, from the perspective of the characters. In their world of "desperation," they have no sense of humor, at least concerning this case.

Questions for the Actors

If Andrew has a partial victory here—outmaneuvering Barry as he lists "evidence" from the past—should the actor adopt the more stylized behavior of the courtroom lawyer? Does his tone change as he shouts down his partner who tries to punctuate his diatribe (in the dialogue printed to the right of his "case" in the script)? Does he deliver his lines here in a "voice" that is different from the more intimate way the two partners have talked to each other earlier in the play?

To what degree is each aware that the objective here has changed from the right-or-wrong/yes-or-no axis of taking Kevin's fraudulent suit to their own personal rivalry? Does Andrew feel like the little brother who now has a victory, however temporary, over Barry—Mister Know-it-all, Mister Always-right? Might the actor deepen Andrew's victory here by calling up an affective or emotional memory from his own life? Would it provide a darker contrast to the joke about the woman with the exploding boobs, and thereby a transition to the next stage?

Objective–Obstacle: Stage Three

Andrew, fresh from a partial victory—let's grant him that much—now tries to go beyond the case at hand. He follows up the general "thought" by appealing to their mutual dislike of "some behemoth of an insurance company" that Tesco might hire, then adds that the supermarket chain, like any other big business, pay their employees low wages.

Questions for the Actors

Do the two bond here for a moment in their hatred of big corporations and the successful lawyers who earn ten times their salaries by representing them? Does that mutual hatred come from a failure to make the grade as corporate lawyers, their being forced to open up a grimy storefront personal injury practice to get by? To what degree does each see failure as imposed by society or fate, or as the sign of personal inadequacy and hence responsibility?

If they bond here, do the two actors come closer together, referencing their reminiscence earlier in the play about being boyhood friends? Do they pull away only when Barry challenges Andrew's claim to have "thought" about the larger justifications for taking Kevin's suit?

Is their mutual delivery here more natural, less agitated, and hence less rhetorical—the informal style they usually adopt when playing with an idea, reviewing a case, or talking about their private lives?

Objective–Obstacle: Stage Four

This is like that moment in the ring when the two fighters, exhausted, hang on to each other, each scoring small ineffective jabs at their opponent. For Barry, Andrew's support of Kevin's case can't be the result of such abstract thought, as he's only just approached them to take his suit; Andrew's somewhat illogical rejoinder is that he couldn't have initiated the idea, for, if he had, he would have "spruced it up a bit." Then—to continue the fight analogy—he pushes back from his opponent and argues this is "the compensation culture"[67] that exists, the world in which little men like them have no choice in the matter. He closes this exchange with a sophomoric argument: Everyone else does it, so why shouldn't they?

Questions for the Actors

Does Barry walk away, perhaps smugly (he's asserting his intellectual superiority, his lawyer's skill in counterargument), when he throws the fact in Andrew's face that Kevin just approached them on the scheme, and Andrew can have had no time for thought? Is he now laughing at his partner?

Andrew follows him with a pleading "Oh come off it, Barry" (subtext: "Come on, give me a little leeway here. The scheme wasn't entirely, not even initially, mine"). Or, does Andrew adopt a sudden change in tactics, the command "come off it" followed by what we have identified as the illogical argument about "sprucing up the claim"?

Are the characters aware of how far they've moved from the initial dispute, for Kevin's fraudulent claim is no longer the central issue: at issue now is their relationship, their sense of themselves, their integrity in a world that Andrew defines as a "culture" that "exists," a system irrespective of human will or desires. The obstacle that they each initially pursued, converting an opponent, has morphed into a complaint about an indifferent society that leaves limits and thereby defines what they can do, what they are.

Objective–Obstacle: Stage Five

The exchange has its own coda. Not denying he's been part of those suits in the past about which he, at the very least, had a "creeping suspicion," Barry reminds Andrew that Scorpion Claims is his firm, an assertion of power and right that unintentionally, even comically, mocks what both would claim is the oppressive authority of the supermarket chain and their lawyers. Each now asserts a power that, however important to them, is petty and no less pathetic from the audience's perspective. Andrew reminds Barry that he inherited the firm only because its previous owner died, while Barry counters by telling his partner that, without him, he'd be out of a job.

The dark humor of the encounter, a microcosm for that of the play, is rooted in a quarrel that leaves both exhausted, both losers but absurdly dependent.

Questions for the Actors

If this is indeed a coda of exhaustion, how do the characters feel about each other now? How strong is the bitterness of the earlier clashes? How resigned are they to an argument of their opponent that they cannot entirely dismiss? Do they move closer physically onstage? Are they possibly aware of making the same assertions they both have used numerous times in the past, albeit under different circumstances? How do the two actors convey—by tone, delivery, gesture, facial expression—that there is something here of what we called in a director's note "a quiet, autumnal quality in the mood"?

The next scene, late in the play, after the judge has ruled in Kevin's favor, is between Andrew and his former lover, Kevin's wife Jennifer. In a curious way, even though they still love each other, they become, for a time, each other's obstacles: each has made a decision about their lives that excludes, or rather may exclude, the other: Jennifer to remain with Kevin, despite everything that has happened; Andrew to quit his present life and move to London. But there are other obstacles involved—namely, Andrew's contempt for the life that Jennifer seems resigned to lead, one he finds shallow, materialistic, and built on lies and compromises. To her, he is a snob, tainted by his profession, even if he is giving it up. They will overcome these obstacles, but without necessarily achieving what they desire. The play ends without a clear resolution, with no sudden infusion of truth, a staple of both sentimental romances and generic court trials.

Andrew Why the fuck d'ya marry him, Jen?
Jennifer *gasps/snorts/laughs, taken aback.*
Jennifer Sort of a question's that?
Andrew He's a fucking arsehole.
Jennifer Yeah. Well. Take one to know one, doesn't it?
Andrew When I heard you two were together, I was fucking gutted.
Jennifer What on earth is that supposed to mean?
Andrew For you. I was fucking gutted for you.
Jennifer That's because you're a snob.
Andrew Just never imagined you'd end up . . .
Jennifer What?
Andrew Doesn't matter.

Jennifer No, go on, what? You never imagined I'd end up what?

Andrew Working in M&S with two fucking kids.

Jennifer Fuck's that supposed to mean?

Andrew You coulda done anything.

Jennifer I *wanted* to have children, Andrew.

Andrew Did you?

Jennifer Reckon you must be in shock or something.

Andrew You wanted kids, or you wanted kids with him?

Jennifer Both.

Andrew Bullshit.

Jennifer You should know.

Andrew Meaning what?

Jennifer Meaning least I'm not the one who makes a living out of it.

Andrew Kids?

Jennifer "Bullshit."

Andrew Change the record.

[*He denounces people like Kevin, who are materialistic, want to feel significant, then adds "it isn't even their fault. Because 's everywhere."*]

Jennifer Our lives have plenty of meaning, actually. Least we didn't leave and get dragged back and end up hating ourselves for it. I like it here. I like the people.

Andrew Minute ago you said you were fucking leaving?

Jennifer Oh, fuck off back to London.

Beat.

Andrew Where's y' sister live? [*Jennifer has told him she's leaving Kevin and taking the children with her to live with her sister.*]

Jennifer Southampton.

Andrew How long y' thinking of goin' for? (*Beat.*) Jen, how long y' thinking—

Jennifer Dunno.

Beat.

Andrew I'm sorry.

Jennifer No y' not.

Andrew I am. Look at me.

Beat.

Jennifer What y' gonna do now?

Andrew How d'ya mean?

Jennifer Now this place is no more.

Andrew Dunno.

Jennifer What d'ya wanna do?

Andrew Dunno

Beat.

When I was four, I trod on this nail. Went straight through my foot. Screamed, started crying, top of my voice. Dad came rushing out, came charging up to me. He picked me up and he wrapped a navy-blue scarf around my foot. Kept screaming, crying, whole street could hear. Then he says, "Look at me." "Look at me," he says. So I did, I looked at him. I looked him right in the eyes. And I stopped crying.

Jennifer *moves to* **Andrew**, *very close. The sound of rain outside fills the room.* [68]

(Act Three)

Again, let's divide the exchange into parts, marked by changing needs, obstacles, and tactics. What the actors have so far established in their characters is now fleshed out as both personal needs and larger circumstances press on them. This time, we'll pose some general questions for the two actors at the end of the "stages" in their exchange.

Needs, Obstacles, Tactics: Stage One

Initiated by Andrew's question, the opening exchange is both blunt and petty: Andrew's dismissal of Kevin as an "arsehole" and Jennifer's clichéd retort, "Takes one to know one." It's as if the two fighters were dancing around each other, not yet committing themselves to the formal fight.

Needs, Obstacles, Tactics: Stage Two

They jump right to some deeply felt emotions. Using the graphic "gutted" as an adjective (British slang), Andrew confesses he was devastated by Jennifer's marrying Kevin. His need is clear—he desires her. But then he overplays his hand, dismissing her life as nothing but "working in M&S with two fucking kids." It doesn't occur to him that Jennifer is at once romantic and practical: she needs to be loved by Andrew, but without giving up her present situation. His contempt for Kevin is mixed with frustration toward himself for taking on a fraudulent claim—indeed, "fifty" or "sixty" of them, by Kevin's estimate.[69] We have a grimly comic situation in which two characters sharing a single basic objective—to be loved by the other—are hampered by Andrew's self-righteous notion of what constitutes a meaningful life and Jennifer's need to justify hers. When we examine, below, Kevin's monologue in court, we'll see that she and her husband have at least that—a need to justify—in common.

Needs, Obstacles, Tactics: Stage Three

Jennifer wins this round, telling Andrew what he already knows, and even using his word "bullshit" against him: a low-life solicitor processing fraudulent car accident cases, he makes a living out of bullshit, lies.

There is break here, "an instance," in the words of one reviewer, "of thesis mongering [which sullies] the 29-year-old dramatist's otherwise blithe touch."[70] Andrew contends that it isn't their fault that "people like Kevin" (does this include Jennifer and himself too?) lead meaningless lives. Rather, he sees them as victims of a system, at once social, economic, and political, beyond their control, or even comprehension.

After his outburst, the exchange with Jennifer leads to three short, related stages, as if the earlier wide-open confrontation had suddenly narrowed, even dissolved.

Needs, Obstacles, Tactics: Stage Four

Andrew, perhaps mostly out of self-interest, asks Jennifer where her sister lives—which is in Southampton, some distance from Kevin. Then he presses the issue of how long she will be there. She gives a noncommittal "Dunno"—coy, enticing. The actor might consider as a subtext: "Does it depend on how things progress between us?"

Needs, Obstacles, Tactics: Stages Five and Six

There follows a fast exchange during which she challenges his apology and he insists he is honest, asking, possibly begging her to "look at" him. Then, she turns the tables: Where is he going now that Scorpion Claims is no more? What is he going to do with his life? Andrew echoes her ambiguous response: "Dunno."

With the playwright's hand evident, Andrew recalls a moment of his father's comforting him when, as a child, he stepped on a nail that "went straight through [his] foot." The father simply asked his son to "look" at him, Andrew's own words to Jennifer when she doubted his "I'm sorry." The play ends with a stage direction: Jennifer moves to Andrew, "*very close*," as the sound of rain outside "*fills the room*."

Questions for the Actors

Imagine Jennifer's life before the play. What might contribute to her conflicted state wherein she cherishes children, finds Kevin less than adequate, still loves Andrew, and yet resists him? Does she see herself as a victim, chained, as he contends, to a meaningless job? How aware is she of those external forces controlling her? Is her calling his job as a personal injury lawyer "bullshit" a matter of self-defense or conviction, or both? What was their love life like, before the play? Why did they break up, and why did she choose Kevin? A director friend liked to say that when you take the stage as a character, you need to know where you are coming from, not just literally but also psychologically.

If Jennifer strikes a chord with the audience, if she is not just some object for our pity but also for our sympathy, so that in her we see something of ourselves, are there moments when the actor can contribute to such identification? Essentially, is the quarrel more than just some isolated petty argument? How does this "domestic" scene, albeit related to the otherwise central event of the play, the fraudulent law suit and the subsequent court trial, allow the actor playing Andrew to adjust his style of delivery toward an expression of the potential "reunion" of former lovers? Does he have here a voice we have not fully heard so far in the play? The trial is over, Barry and Kevin are out of the picture; how can the two actors, by voice, subtext, and movement, link this exchange to the larger play, make it something more than just an appendage or moment that seems "underwritten," as David Benedict has suggested?[71]

After that sociological critique of the compensation culture, the tension mostly dissipates in stages four, five, and six above. How can the actors show this through what we have called, in Chapter 3, "body awareness"; the way they hold themselves, move onstage, and relate physically to each other with gestures that will contrast with their earlier angry confrontation? How do we get from petty and therefore comic (from our perspective) quarreling to the qualified romance, the sentiment at the end, punctuated musically by "*the sound of the rain outside* [that] *fills the room*"?

The Same Deep Water as Me ends with Kevin out of the picture (his idea of becoming a "team" with Andrew and Barry is rejected, after which he is physically attacked by Andrew). Barry and Andrew mostly reconcile over a meal (take-out Asian food, with a cake shaped like a scorpion); the firm has been dissolved, the two partners are about to lead new lives. Jennifer and Andrew, despite their mutual "dunno"s, may get back together. If not the happy ending of conventional comedy, Payne offers a partial, ambiguous, possible resolution, quite in line with the atmosphere of a dark, if not a black, comedy.

Objectives, Obstacles, Needs — and Comedy

In this final section, we consider a monologue within which the character is only partially aware of the obstacles he faces, whether inflicted by society or himself. Not always conscious of his objective, Kevin is at once pathetic and comic. At this stage in the play, the contradictions and therefore fabrications in his testimony have been exposed in court. The defense lawyer, Georgina Burns, has called his bluff about the alleged car crash on two issues. She asks why his first instinct was not to attend to his child in the backseat, rather than getting out of the car and confronting the other driver (of course, despite the story concocted by his lawyers, neither the child nor his mother were actually there). The second issue concerns his inability to justify his family going on a week's vacation the day after the accident, before even taking the (supposedly) injured child to a doctor.

Here we confront a stance born of desperation and that pervades the play, the insane mixture of self-interest, fear, objectives both conscious and unconscious, a fierce desire to satisfy some need that the character in question cannot fully define, a contempt for what he labels an oppressive society that in turn becomes a justification of behavior that we see as at once understandable but comic, illogical, not fully thought through (recall that Andrew and Barry quibble on the word "thought"). Kevin spews out a wild collage of emotions, the comic bravado of a cat cornered, the faulty vision of a powerless person who thinks a brief moment of dubious success will go on forever. There are several possible takes on the monologue as it progresses, and so, without being prescriptive, we suggest in brackets before each beat the emotional stance an actor *might* consider:

> **Kevin** [*A feigned indifference to what others think:*] Look if you wanna fucking *harangue* me for not looking after Luce, then, fine, y'know, fine. [*A less-than-earnest confession of relativity, the "it's just your perspective" dodge:*] Fair enough. [*An insincere apology, or half apology, wherein his speech falters:*] Maybe I was a bit mean, maybe I was a bit, fucking, dismissive. [*A parody of lawyer's logic, ironic since the child and his mother were not present during the accident, coupled with a reason that makes no sense, does not follow logically:*] But I don't really see what that has to do with the fact that, actually, y'know, fucking, actually, that the main reason for us not sorta fucking doing anything about it, is cos we didn't wanna make a fucking fuss! [*Now just an emotional outburst, as if that would elicit sympathy, maybe even understanding:*] And fucking grilling me and fucking grilling me— [*Trying to put the blame on the system:*] I mean whass y' fucking problem? [*Now the cry of envy from the disenfranchised, a pseudo-Marxist blaming of capitalism— this may not be entirely wrong, but is surely beyond Kevin's comprehension:*] I mean how much fucking— No I mean I'm being serious, how much fucking money d'you lot make? [*Retreating to the absolutism of "end of story," even though it is based on the fiction that the accident was real:*] *She* shunted into the back of *us*. End of story.[72]
>
> (Act Two)

These are good starting points for the actor to use to develop the psychological states, the shifts in tone and delivery, the aspects of character, the gaps between Kevin's conscious tactics and our larger subtextual reading of his character in order to bring the nuances of his character forward.

Principles and Perceptions of Comedy

As we have seen in this final chapter, the genre of "comedy" is really a series of subgenres including farce, physical comedy, romantic or sentimental comedy, and social–political comedy. These four, of course, hardly exhaust the list of possible ways in which a playwright can perceive the world through laughter. There are also basic rules, principles of performance, governing all comedies, and then there are those specific to the subgenres, which is why we considered different approaches for the actor with the four modern plays considered here.

* * *

In the Coda following, we turn to a factor in comic theatre that has, both explicitly and implicitly, been our subject all along and is as important as the actor or the playwright: the audience. Their presence ratifies the comedy and their laughter is its goal, from a simple reaction to a joke to that more profound response when the comedy touches something of vital importance to the spectator in the house. As we like to tell our theatre majors, actors onstage performing to an empty house are not in a play but only rehearsing, and a crowd sitting in the house watching an empty stage is just a crowd and not an audience, as that term applies to the vital collaboration between those on- and offstage. So, since we have been talking throughout this book about the audience, the goal of the comic actor, our final comments will, as befits a coda, be brief.

Notes

1 Richard Bean, *One Man, Two Guvnors: Based on "The Servant of Two Masters" by Carlo Goldoni* (London: Oberon Books, 2011).
2 Henry Lewis, Jonathan Sayer, and Henry Shields, *The Play That Goes Wrong*, 3rd ed. (London: Bloomsbury, 2015).
3 Tim Firth, *Calendar Girls* (London: Samuel French, 2010).
4 Nick Payne, *The Same Deep Water as Me* (London: Faber and Faber, 2013).
5 Bean, *One Man, Two Guvnors*, 13.
6 Ibid., 29.
7 Ibid., 13.
8 Ibid., 22.
9 Ibid., 15.

10 Ibid., 19.
11 Ibid., 29.
12 Ibid., 61.
13 Ibid., 81.
14 Ibid., 42.
15 Ibid., 48.
16 Ibid., 55.
17 Ibid., 74–5.
18 Ibid., 77–8.
19 Ibid., 27.
20 Ibid., 64.
21 Ibid., 67.
22 Ibid., 68.
23 Ibid., 19.
24 Ibid., 31.
25 Ibid., 35–6.
26 Ibid., 62.
27 Ibid., 65.
28 Ibid., 12.
29 Ibid., 42.
30 Ibid., 88.
31 Ibid., 68–9.
32 Ibid., 83.
33 Ibid., 73.
34 See, for example, Nimax Theatres, *The Play That Goes Wrong*, http://
    www.nimaxtheatres.com/duchess-theatre/the_play_that_goes_wrong
    (accessed June 7, 2016); Tim Walker, "*The Play That Goes Wrong*,
    Duchess Theatre, review: 'delightful,'" *The Daily Telegraph*, September
    18, 2014, http://www.telegraph.co.uk/culture/theatre/theatre-reviews/
    11106181/The-Play-That-Goes-Wrong-Duchess-Theatre-review-
    delightful.html (accessed June 7, 2016); and Mark Shenton, review of
    The Play that Goes Wrong, *London Theatre Guide*, September 15, 2014,
    https://www.londontheatre.co.uk/reviews/the-play-that-goes-wrong-
    review (accessed June 7, 2016).
35 Lewis, Sayer, and Shields, *The Play That Goes Wrong*, 5.
36 Ibid., 6.
37 Ibid., 17.
38 Ibid., 57.
39 Ibid., 16.
40 Ibid., 53.
41 Ibid., 58.
42 Ibid., 65.
43 Ibid., 70.
44 Ibid., 71.

45 Ibid.
46 Ibid., 27.
47 Ibid., 43.
48 Ibid., 46.
49 Ibid.
50 Harold Pinter, *The Lover*, in *Harold Pinter: Complete Works*, vol. 2
    (New York: Grove Press, 1990), 159–96.
51 Pinter, *The Lover*, 161.
52 Firth, *Calendar Girls*.
53 Ibid., vi.
54 Ibid., 2.
55 Ibid., 4.
56 Ibid.
57 Ibid., 5.
58 Ibid., 6.
59 Ibid., 7.
60 Ibid., 9.
61 Ibid.
62 Ibid.
63 Ibid., 10.
64 Ibid., 11.
65 Ibid.
66 Payne, *The Same Deep Water as Me*, 59–61.
67 Matt Wolf, "Nick Payne's Latest Play Takes Him in a New Direction,"
    review of *The Same Deep Water as Me*, *New York Times*, August 20,
    2013, http://www.nytimes.com/2013/08/21/arts/Nick-Paynes-latest-
    play-takes-him-in-a-new-direction.html?_r=0 (accessed September
    1, 2015).
68 Payne, *The Same Deep Water as Me*, 109–11.
69 Ibid., 102.
70 Wolf, "Nick Payne's Latest Play Takes Him in a New Direction."
71 David Benedict, "London Legit Review: *The Same Deep Water as Me*,"
    Variety, August 13, 2013, http://variety.com/2013/legit/reviews/london-
    legit-review-the-same-deep-water-as-me-1200575363/ (accessed June
    10, 2016).
72 Payne, *The Same Deep Water as Me*, 76–7.

CODA: THE AUDIENCE

The art and craft of comedy, its aesthetics and its enactment, are inseparable and of equal interest to both actor and spectator as collaborators in the performance. As we've observed, the audience for comedy is present in the way that the audience for, say, *Hamlet* is not. Comedic actors hope to hear the audience's response, the ultimate expression of which is their laughter, whether soft or ear-shattering, subdued or demonstrative. The comedic actor will surely want to do everything he can to generate this. The audience's parallel presence and importance for the performance, epitomized in their laughter, is what jazz musicians would call a rim shot, that musical riff underscoring and justifying what the artist is doing. Brecht was right in that there is a good reason for keeping lights on in the house: it calls attention to the two vital elements of the performance—actor and audience.

The Renaissance commentator William Webb defined the purpose of art as allowing an audience to "gather together and keep company and keep fellowship together."[1] Comedy does this, uniting those onstage and in the house; in this way, the genre is affirmative, positive, even erring on the side of optimism, whether black comedy or farce, sentimental or purely physical. In laughing at the actors and their characters, do we not laugh at ourselves, at the character or characters we play in real life, consciously so in moments of clarity and self-reflection as well as unconsciously so, perhaps too often, when we lose perspective on ourselves—but then, this is where comedy can provide a restorative mirror. In believing in his comic character, the actor with his craft invites us to believe in him. And when the comedy is over, perhaps we carry outside the theatre that pleasure in a convincing illusion.

The ultimate goal of this book, no less than that of a comedy and its performance, is to better enable actors to reach an audience and play the characters. From the stage, the goal is to get a reaction, to involve the audience in an illusive comedic world and—to use that single word endemic to comedy—to make them *laugh*. As do some of the plays we reference, we address two audiences here that are at length one. Our audience is both actors wanting to perfect their skills as comedic actors and general readers who like to go the theatre, like to see comedies, and like to laugh.

For the actor, we have offered a variety of rules, suggestions, tips, and principles to guide him as he moves from getting cast, to the read-through, to rehearsals, and to opening night. He will want to carefully examine the text to which he must be faithful as he devises a subtext to deepen his character. The playwright's creative process is matched by the equally creative process of the actor, influenced by that of his fellow actors, and perhaps enhanced by improv games and exercises.

Furthermore, the reader, not so swept up into the comic world that he thinks it real, always aware it is a play, no matter how compelling, is made more aware of the craft of the actor. Here's the paradox: the more skilled the actor in creating an illusion, the more he draws attention to the craft. So, learning more about the craft of the comedic actor only enhances the experience of our reader in the audience. In the simplest of equations, the art of comedy coexists with the craft, the performance itself. We offer these notes in the hope of balancing this equation.

Note

1 William Webb, "A Discourse of English Poetrie," in *Elizabethan Critical Essays*, vol. 1, ed. G. Gregory Smith (London: Oxford University Press, 1904), 234.

INDEX